Praise for *Follow Your YES*

"Ken Bechtel has been a dear friend for more than 20 years, and it's fantastic to see his humor and deep wisdom distilled into such a wonderful book. Ken has a way of flowing through life that I'd never seen before and a way of making challenging things feel easy and doable.

I remember when we first started teaching together in 2003. I was nervous before our first intuition class and showed up with pages of printed notes and an outline timed to the minute. When I asked Ken if he was ready, he flashed me a confident smile, said "Yes!" and pulled out a tiny yellow sticky note with a few words scratched on it.

I thought he was joking (Ken is incredibly funny) but that was really how he'd prepared. He was confident in his first step and brave enough to take it, and as it turns out that was enough ... both for our classes and for life itself.

In *Follow Your YES* Ken shares his strategy for living life easily and rolling with life's changes. One of Ken's great gifts is making complex information simple and accessible, and this book is no exception. Ken draws on his experiences and speaks from his heart in a way that inspires you to do the same—to listen to your heart and live the experiences you desire."

—**Jeffrey Allen**, Founder of Spirit Mind Living and
Author of *Mindvalley's Duality Energy Training*

"*Follow Your YES* is a wonderful, inspirational book that will change your life! Ken Bechtel gives you simple steps to gain confidence, take your life to the next level that calls to you, and be happier in the process!"

—**Dr. Diana Kirschner**, bestselling author of *Love in 90 Days*

"If you struggle with uncertainty, the principles in this book can free you. *Follow Your YES* is a simple recipe to enhance your life. When you apply the simple formula Ken provides for going from YES to YES to YES and being your best, you can achieve life-changing results."

—**Christy Whitman**, New York Times bestselling author and master coach

"That still small voice always knows what is right for us, but getting to it is the challenge. With *Follow Your YES*, Ken not only introduces us to our superpower, he teaches us how to harness it to create the life we are meant to live. Ken breaks down that process into understandable practical and spiritual steps. You will never look at choice the same way. What a profound book."

—**Mark J. Silverman**, Best selling author of *Only 10s 2.0*

"You have yourself a YES from me and the Universe."

—**Mary Bell Nyman**, Founder and retired
Director of Psychic Horizons Center

"Ken has written a wonderful guide to *Following Your YES*, which is helpful for all those who are facing a fork in the road, especially in midlife. The book is a great reminder of how I followed my own crazy YES in 2009 that led me to an entirely new creative career in theater"

—**Wendy Gillespie**, President and CEO Starhawk Productions

"We live in a world of logical and rational decisions. We often need to have our plans mapped out well in advance of taking action. We think these provide the safest route to where we want to go ... but what if the safest route is exactly the opposite? Following your intuition, trusting the messages that say "go here and don't go there," and surrendering to the path that unfolds when you take just one step, one YES, at a time. In *Follow Your YES*, Ken Bechtel shares his deep wisdom and personal experience of living life guided by YES. Even if you're a spiritual skeptic like me, you'll find yourself curious about what might be possible, and you'll walk away with practical steps for experimenting with what following YES could look like for you."

—**Dr. Erin Baker**, Self-Leadership Coach and author of *Joy-full AF: The Essential Business Strategy We're Afraid To Put First*

Follow Your YES

Follow Your YES

A Simple Idea to Improve Anyone's Life

KEN BECHTEL

Follow Your YES: A Simple Idea to Improve Anyone's Life

Book design and cover: Michelle Radomski: www.onevoicecan.com

Paperback: 979-8-9863798-1-4
eBook: 979-8-9863798-0-7
Library of Congress Control Number: 2022911714

KenBechtel.com

To all those who are ready to follow their YES.
Your commitment to being the best you can be
and enhance the world with your gifts is an inspiration.

- KB

Contents

Prologue

My friend Kurt is an amazing artist and creator. He's a painter, sculptor, furniture designer, and musician. I always look forward to speaking with him because we have the most interesting conversations.

Typically, when I go to his home, I've barely stepped inside and we're already in a fascinating discussion. One day several years ago I went to see him and he greeted me with a look of childlike curiosity and wonder on his face and he said, "Ken, I've figured it out. It's either YES or it's NO!"

At first this sounded rather elementary to me, but since I know Kurt can sometimes be rather creative in his thinking, and he is someone who always deeply explores whatever topic he is focused on, I smiled and said, "Yeeaah ... what do you mean?"

He went on to explain that your YES is clear. You just know it.

It's like being handed a menu and instantly knowing what you're going to order without scanning the whole thing. You can *feel* your YES. And everything else is a NO. So, all we are meant to do in life is go from YES to YES to YES. Your YES is sitting there right in front of you waiting for you to embrace it. Waiting for you to **follow your YES,** Kurt told me. I thought on this for minute.

What if following our YES is the key?
What if it is that simple?
What if that is exactly what we're meant to do with our lives?

As simple and enticing as this sounded, I had to chew on it for a while. The more I did, the clearer it became.

If we just pay attention to our YES and act on whatever it is, and then ask, "What is my YES now" and act on that one, we will live a life full of YESES.

Every YES we follow leads to another YES. If we are paying attention, that is.

This feeling of our YES is divine guidance. This is why I am capitalizing YES in this book. It comes from the Universe, God, Allah, Great Spirit, Infinite Intelligence, the Creator, the Divine or whatever you call the higher power. It's the answer we are seeking when we ask for something to "just show me the way." (By the way - I view all these terms for a higher power to be interchangeable, and you will find me using various ones throughout the book. Know that for me these are all referring to the same thing.)

Have you ever gone east to get west? Or right to get left? Why? Because you could see the bigger picture, and it made sense.

Did you know UPS drivers almost never make left turns? They've looked from a more informed perspective, the map from above, to avoid turning across oncoming traffic. They know this saves time, cuts the risk of accidents, and somewhat surprisingly ends up being more fuel efficient.

These delivery drivers know the exact destination they are heading to, but you and I don't necessarily know what our destination is on a given day, week, year or our lifetime. We may have an idea of where we would like to end up, but we don't have a fixed destination. We don't have access to the grand scheme of things, but the Universe does. When you're following your YES, you're trusting that the Universe sees the bigger picture of your life; it knows where your highest good is to be found and exactly how to guide you there.

This happened to me as I was writing this book. I woke up with a clear feeling of YES.

The YES was to stop making excuses for not having finished this book yet. I needed to find a place to work where I wouldn't be distracted and just write. It was like a bug buzzing around that I could no longer ignore, or an itch that needed to be scratched. The first step was to clear my sched open up the time in my calendar. Step two was to send an email at 6:18 a.m. to my friend Suzanne whose house I'm at in Leadville, Colorado as I write.

Good morning.

I woke up with the writing bug and have cleared my schedule for the first part of next week to focus on my book.

What needs to happen or what do I need to know to be able to have your place in Leadville be my writing retreat from this Sunday the 24th through the middle of next week?

I know this is short notice, but for some reason I am being called to focus on writing so I want to honor this calling.

Thank you - Ken

I didn't know how I was going to find a place where I wouldn't be distracted, but I paid attention to my YES first by clearing my schedule. If Suzanne's place had not been available I would have found somewhere else. Following your YES is quite easy when you take the first step and allow the "how" of it coming to fruition to be revealed. (Turns out by following this YES and carving out some time so I wouldn't be distracted, I wrote the entire first draft of this book in just six days.)

My YES right now is this book. Everything in this book is divinely guided. I didn't make this up. My YES is to be a messenger to remind you the Divine is always here for you. The Divine is guiding you to your highest good in the form of a YES. Your YES is that emotional, visceral, attention-grabbing device that provides direction regarding what will help us shine and blossom in our own unique way so we can share our distinctive expression of the Divine with those in our orbit.

If you want an example of a YES, know that every single thing you read in this book, both my personal experiences of following my YES and the words of wisdom that surround them were all divinely guided.

As you proceed through these pages, start to consider what you could accomplish if you were consistently following your YES instead of running around in circles chasing Maybes.

Introduction

For a lot of people these days it can feel like life is running us instead of us running our lives. It's as if the responsibilities and demands of our careers, family and the world-at-large are dragging us around by the tail. I often hear people say, "I don't know when the last time was I did something just for me. I don't think I've ever put myself first." Living this way leads to an empty and unfulfilling life.

Do you ever feel like life is passing you by? Like you are stuck? Are you sitting there wondering when your life is going to start? Is it tiring for you to deny your heart's desires and just keep doing what you think you "should" or following along with what others expect of you?

If you are tired of feeling stuck, unmotivated and uncertain about what to do next, following your YES will set you free.

Are you ready to be excited about your life again and confident in your next steps?

Do you want to feel at ease being yourself instead of worrying about people pleasing all the time?

Are you eager to contribute to the world by sharing your passions?

Following your YES is like tapping into a superpower you didn't know you had. This superpower took me from being totally confused, chasing Maybes and doing what other people were doing because I figured if it worked for them it would work for me, to following my YES day in and day out so I could love my life, trust my heart and be excited about every step I take.

Following your YES is about being your best. Not from a "Look at me. I'm so cool." perspective, but from a commitment to share the best version of yourself with everyone you meet.

Learning how to follow my YES moved me out of overwhelm, uncertainty and procrastination and into the love, prosperity and happiness that comes from living my truth with ease and confidence.

For more than 20 years, I've been helping people honor their voice in their relationships and teaching how to find and follow their YES so they have fulfilling relationships that last. As my work evolved it became clear the practice of following your YES applied to all areas of life and not just to romantic relationships. Over time I developed an analogy that all of us are like a rose trying to bloom. (You'll learn more about this shortly.) For you and me, blooming is more than just beauty, as most people think of when they consider a rose. We could be blooming and opening creatively, emotionally, mentally, spiritually, in our lifestyle, our careers, our passions, or any other number of areas of our life that we are looking to step into more completely. The more I utilized this analogy with my clients I recognized the primary YES for my career is to help the world be filled with blooming roses; with people who are living their fullest expression, who have found their voice, reconnected with their Inner Authority, and are confidently sharing their gifts with the world.

Following your YES is being clear about what you need to be the real you. The you that has been hidden away deep down inside and is dying to get out. What part of you have you been hiding away?

Following your YES requires developing some muscles you probably haven't used in a while. Muscles like the prioritizing-you muscles, speaking-your-truth muscles, connecting-with-your-inner-guidance muscles, and so on. Through lack of use these muscles have atrophied, but they are not gone. You are not starting from scratch. It is much like if you broke your arm and it had to be in a cast for six weeks. When the cast is removed your arm will be all scrawny and weak from lack of use. This is exactly what has happened to the muscles you need to follow your YES and bloom. If you haven't used these muscles, they've become weak. I'm going to show you how to build these muscles up so you can be the strongest you possible.

Full transparency, I'll be using lots of analogies in this book. So, if you love analogies you're in the right place, and even if you are not a big fan of analogies keep reading, because the analogies I'm about to share with you are fresh, unforgettable and life changing. I'm aware that no analogy is perfect, so instead of asking yourself if you agree or don't agree with what I present, ask yourself how this could improve your life. Look for the gold, not the gravel.

You're going to find out a lot more about how to identify and follow your YES as you read on, and you'll come to understand how following your YES — your enthusiasms, your truth — makes life easier and more fun.

Life is a hell of a lot more fun if you follow your yes rather than your no.

- Sir Richard Branson[1]

Be aware you don't have to know HOW you're going to make it happen. When you follow your YES the *how* gets revealed, but only after you've taken the first step of following it.

Once I arrived in Leadville to write my book, I started by doing a search on my computer for all the notes I had made related to the topic. I used "FYY" to tag these files, so I quickly entered FYY in the search bar and hit return.

Up popped something called - FYY 2016 v.1.0. That had been deeply tucked away in the recesses of my hard drive. I had only started thinking of calling the book *Follow Your YES* a couple of months prior to this in 2021, so I wondered what this file from 2016 was all about.

I opened the file and found I'd written an outline for a book called *Follow Your YES* five years before. I was shocked. Back then I had been adamant that I was not a writer and had no interest in writing a book, and yet I had written an outline. Even more interesting was that the outline very closely resembled the book you have in your hands. All this reinforced that I was on the right track and writing this book was indeed my YES.

Your YES is that thing that supports you in blooming. It doesn't matter if it's something you're excited about or that scares you, something that brings you joy or that makes you melancholy. Sometimes your YES is a difficult step to take but in the long run it serves you in being able to bloom. Ending a relationship, changing a lifestyle, or moving on from the past can all bring about levels of sadness and grief however they also free you to stay in alignment with your truth, and your truth always supports you in blooming.

In my opinion, life is like crossing a stream by stepping on stones. The person who crosses quickly and with ease is following one YES after another in present time. Each stone they stepped on was selected only after the previous step was taken. To someone observing from the shore, it looks like they had it all figured out before they started, but this is not true. Trying to figure out all the steps before you start rarely works because once you arrive on a stone, your perspective changes and you see the path in a new way. The stones that looked unsafe from the shore now look solid, and the stones you planned on leaping to next reveal how unstable they are.

Following your YES is an active sport. There is nothing passive about this approach to life. By the end of this book, you will have all the tools you need to identify your best next step so you can enjoy life again. You'll know exactly how to discern between following your YES so everybody wins and chasing Maybes or doing something that is a NO for you because you're afraid you might disappoint somebody (which ends up disappointing yourself).

You're going to get crystal clear on how to connect with your YES. We'll demystify all the other things you have been following instead of your YES, like your NOs and Maybes, and how they're holding you back. Plus, I will walk you through the exact formula I use every day for following my YES.

So, if you are ready to reclaim your power, make more confident decisions, and feel excited about life again, let's get started.

Your YES

Hopefully you are reading this book because it was a YES for you. Not because someone said you *should* read it or that you must read it. If this book was recommended to you, I hope you found something inside of you that confirmed this is the next book for you to read. If this is true for you, then you listened to and are now following your YES. Congratulations!

— 1 —

THE ROSE

As I mentioned earlier, during my 20-plus years of helping clients follow their YES and find their voice in relationships I developed an analogy that each of us is like a rose who is here to bloom. Oftentimes, when I speak with people about following their YES, they'll admit they don't even know what their YES would be. They're so distant from feeling aligned with their purpose and their reason for being here that the whole idea of following their YES seems unattainable. If you can relate, please know you're not alone.

Most people hear "follow your YES" and assume this is about your life purpose, your deeply meaningful reason for getting out of bed in the morning. We expect it to look like leaving a thriving corporate career to start a charity to feed the poor, or adopting orphans from a war-torn country, or dedicating your life to finding a cure for cancer. In western culture we often connect the idea of life purpose to our vocation.

Let me be crystal clear: Your YES, as I talk about it in this book, is NOT your life purpose. There's no pressure to be clear on your ultimate contribution or destination in life. Give yourself permission to let your YES be as uncomplicated as honoring who you are in this moment and what you need to grow. Are you willing to permit yourself this freedom?

Once you start following your YES, you'll increase your confidence, reclaim your energy, stop sabotaging your heart, plus you'll enjoy more peace of mind and freedom in all areas of your life by blooming into the rose you are here to be.

Fear not, all this talk about blooming like a rose is not about turning you into a flower. It is simply an analogy to help illustrate how following your YES impacts how you show up in the world. Here's how this rose analogy came to light for me.

I was 33 years old, living in Portland, Oregon and taking a photography class with my friend Peter, who you will meet later. Early one morning I drove to the International Rose Test Garden to try my hand at photographing flowers. Even though there are beautiful flowers all over Portland, I figured this would be the ideal place to start since they have over 10,000 rose bushes in one place. Walking around this garden with thousands of rose bushes was a breathtaking experience.

What amazed me was virtually all the roses were blooming at once. I wondered how this happened. "How do they all bloom at once," I asked one of the caretakers. "How does this work? How do you make nearly 650 different varieties of roses blossom at once?"

"It's not easy," he replied, and he went on to explain how every one of the roses has its own unique combination of needs that must be met for it to bloom. Some need more water, others respond well to direct sunlight and still others react best to indirect sunlight, and they all need a unique blend of nutrients. Because they each receive precisely what they need, they all bloom.

Then he corrected me on something and pointed out that all of the roses weren't blooming at once. When I looked closely, I could see there were some rose bushes with no blossoms at all, they were just thorny green plants. There were others with buds but no blooms.

The caretaker told me they all have the potential to blossom once they get their needs met, but some take longer than others. Once they have the right combination of sunlight, water, nutrients and space to grow in, they will bloom. He added, "The blooms are their gifts to the world."

Now here is the really cool part. As I was walking through this sea of roses, just taking it all in, I totally forgot I was there to take pictures. I noticed a particular rose that was pink and orange and yellow all melded together. I always think of it as being the color of the chewable baby aspirin my Mom gave me when I was a child. It even smelled like baby aspirin to me. (I really loved those aspirin because they were orange-flavored and I thought they were yummy.) As soon as I saw this rose I realized it was my favorite. Out of 650 varieties, this one most resonated for me. It was clear this was my rose and I immediately wanted to contribute to making sure it continued to bloom.

I also noticed that no one was stopping to admire bushes that weren't blooming. The rose bushes with no blooms at all or those with just buds on them may as well have been invisible. Without blooming there was no way for me to know if they were a "baby aspirin" rose that I adored, nor could anyone else tell if they were their favorite variety. Blooming and sharing their gifts was the key to being loved and adored.

Some people bloom late. Some very late.
And some, very, very, super late. But they all bloom.
And the longer it takes, the more spectacular it is.
The best is yet to come.[2]

- The Universe

Every one of us has the potential to bloom into our own version of a breathtaking rose. No matter who you are or where you came from, every person has this potential. To do this it's helpful to identify which stage of blooming you are currently in:

- Are you a thorny green plant? A rose bush with no blooms or buds on it? You lack confidence and are indecisive. Your gifts are hidden away, you're uncomfortable fully expressing yourself, and you feel like you're a long way from blooming and thriving.
- Are you a budding rose bush? It's clear you have potential. You're better than you used to be at making choices and speaking your truth, but you're still not fully opening and sharing your gifts and your passions with confidence.

- Or are you a fully blooming rose bush? Are you confidently sharing your unique gifts with the world, and no longer doubting yourself? Are you blossoming for no other reason than it is who you are, and as a result are you being admired by many and truly loved by the select few who would bend over backwards to do what it takes to support you in continuing to bloom?

There is no wrong answer. I simply want you to be fully aware, as we get started, of where you're at in the blooming process and how much you are currently sharing who you truly are with your sphere of influence.

How did the rose ever open its heart
and give to this world all of its beauty?
It felt the encouragement of light against its being,
otherwise we all remain too frightened.

- St. Thomas Aquinas[3]

Your YES is your guide to blooming. You bloom because it is who you are. It's not situational, it is essential. Your bloom is your essence being shared with the world. Your true colors, your flair, your intelligence, your abilities, your strengths and your brilliance.

When you're following your YES
you build confidence
and eliminate competition.

— 2 —

Why Is Your YES Important?

There are countless reasons why following your YES is important. Let me give you the three biggest payoffs I have found in my years of this practice.

First, **following your YES eliminates overwhelm.**

One of the most common things I hear from people is how overwhelmed they feel. There's so much going on in their lives, so much to do and they continually feel like they're running behind. You might feel this way sometimes as well.

One of the greatest payoffs of following your YES is that it eliminates overwhelm.

When you are doing exactly what you're divinely guided to do in this moment you will feel peace.

When you follow your YES you experience a feeling of relief. The tension disappears because you're honoring you. Following your YES releases you from the weight of the big "R." This is the burden we take on for feeling responsible for others' experiences. Clients have told me it's that same feeling you get when you address the elephant in the room. When you follow your YES you're addressing the elephant in your heart.

Following your YES makes the feeling of overwhelm a thing of the past because you are no longer getting caught up in all the activities and tasks that aren't really yours in this moment.

In fact when you feel overwhelmed, it is an indicator you are not following your YES. More than likely you are chasing Maybes and this is why it feels so overwhelming.

My friend Maggie told me about something she calls Angel Trips which are a great demonstration of how following our YES in the moment eliminates overwhelm.

At the time she discovered this Maggie was a single mom with two young boys who were 4- and 6-years-old. The idea of planning and preparing everything required to take a trip with the boys was overwhelming, so instead they would simply get in the car, pull out of the driveway and then rotate through each of them choosing where to turn next. They followed their YESES and as Maggie put it, "let the angels guide them." She always packed their tent, sleeping bags, and a cooler of food and water so at nightfall if they were somewhere without accommodations, they'd have food and someplace to sleep. This eliminated worries about where they would stay, whether they would get there "on time," or if she'd picked the right place to go. Not only did she tell me they found some of the most extraordinary places that they never would have come across if she had planned everything ahead of time, but by focusing on doing only what she was guided to do in the moment, taking the boys on trips was something she looked forward to instead of dreaded.

Payoff #1 is the elimination of overwhelm.

The second major payoff of following your YES: **it removes competition.**

When you are authentic and following your YES, there is no competition. You are always the one who is the best at being yourself. No one could ever say to you, "There are two other people who are better at being you than you are." That's impossible.

As legendary actress Judy Garland[4] put it, "Always be a first-rate version of yourself, instead of a second-rate version of somebody else."

Imitators are never better at being the original than the original itself. This is why we rarely remember cover bands. Instead we remember who they are covering and imitating. It's when we're trying to be like others, or we're comparing ourselves to others, or thinking others know what's best for us that we become less than who we are really here to be.

In the movie *Ray* about the life of music legend Ray Charles, there is a scene where Ray is on a date with Della Bea Antoine, the woman who would become his wife. He asks her if she has heard his new song and what did she think of it.

She says, "It's nice, but I feel like I have heard it before. I keep wondering what the real Ray Charles sounds like."

You can see he is deeply impacted by this comment and tries to brush it off by saying, "Ray Charles, who's he?"

To which she replies, "No one if you don't know." At that time Ray believed since he was blind his only option for making a living was to imitate other performers. Later, as they are walking home he says, "When you're blind, Miss Antoine, you ain't got that many choices."

She takes this in for a moment and then says, "Seem to me like you got all the choices in the world. God gave you the gift to sound like anybody you please, even yourself."

Ray Charles started his career by mimicking famous performers of the day, and he made a decent living doing this, but it was not until he stopped copying others, followed his YES and brought forth his original sound that his career really took off. Once he embraced his unique abilities and brought forward his originality, only then did the legend we know today simply as "Ray" come into being.

Ray Charles had no competition because no one else could be him. This is true for all of us.

Your influence resides in your originality! Your originality and influence are your unique capacities, which are set free when you follow your YES.

You were born an original. Don't die a copy![5]

- John Mason

When I tell the story of me finding the "baby aspirin" rose that I knew was my rose, I'm often asked why I connected with this particular rose?

The truth is wanting to know why I connected with the 'baby aspirin" rose is simply a desire to know what you can do to be like that rose so you get picked. This is a very natural question, but here's the thing, it doesn't matter, because you cannot be that rose. What matters is that you be the fullest expression of yourself, so you can be admired for being you, and it doesn't matter if you are a rose, a petunia, a tulip or a cactus.

Your task is to put your energy into blooming so you can be recognized for who you are and attract the people who love your blooms and choose you ... the real you. This is the same for your personal, professional or your love life.

Trying to be like another rose will never attract your best match. It will simply put you in competition with another rose and require you to invest tons of effort and energy to imitate it, instead of relaxing into being you.

The best part is there's no competition when we follow our YES because then we're presenting our unique bloom. No rose is a match for everyone, but every rose has someone, many someones, they match who can't wait to support them in continuing to blossom. The key to finding that someone is for you to bloom. The rest will take care of itself.

Following your YES is what allows you to live the fullest, richest, most delicious life possible. And as a result, you get to share your glorious uniqueness with the rest of us.

To do this you have to be motivated by your truth. It has to be your reason for doing it.

You can easily get caught up in thinking that since your friend lost 10 pounds and then they found this great romantic partner, this must mean you just need to lose 10 pounds, and then you'll attract a great romantic partner too.

The problem is that losing 10 pounds is not your truth, it's theirs. It's not your YES.

This is you trying to be like your friend to have the results they had. This will never work. You must be authentically **you** in order to have the results that align, support and honor you. Your motivation must come from what's true for you *right now*.

When you're following your YES you build confidence and eliminate competition. By sharing your unique expression of the Divine you make it easier for your fans to find you. Which is a pretty good payoff, don't you think?

The third way following your YES is important: **it leads you to attract the people, situations and opportunities that match you.** Let me show you a couple of different ways this can play out:

I worked with wonderful woman named Jane who had recently gone through a divorce. We were talking about needs and what she needed to be her best right then. I asked her, "What is your YES in this moment." Her answer was books.

> She said, *You know, when I came here, I parked at the library across the street, and as I was walking over here, I was reminded how much I love books. I've always loved to read. Libraries are one of my favorite places.*
>
> *But when I was married, we had children and I always felt like I couldn't go get books for me. I needed to get them for the kids. I would never go to the library by myself because I felt like I should have been taking the kids. Then when I took the kids, I never looked for myself. I only checked out books for them.*
>
> *I don't know where that came from,* she said. *I literally gave up something very meaningful to me. I could have been a mom who read and was a great role model to my children of how fun and important reading was instead of trying to force them to read when they never saw me reading.*
>
> The next time I saw Jane she said, *Ken, you won't believe what happened. After class I went back to my car, and thought why don't I go to the library now? So that's what I did.*
>
> *As I walked in the door I had this feeling of, "Oh my God, I've missed this place."*

I started looking around at all my favorite authors then I noticed, out of the corner of my eye, a person coming down the aisle and as he drew nearer he said, "Hey, Jane, how are you doing?"

Turns out it was a guy I knew from work. We chatted a little bit and discovered we enjoyed many of the same authors and genres. We decided to go have a coffee, and on the way out I checked out a couple books, just for me, for the first time in years.

I was so excited to have satisfied my love of books in this way, and on top of that as we were finishing up our coffees, he asked me out, and we've started dating.

She said, *This whole time I was worried how I would move forward in my life and meet someone. Turns out I just needed to be me, so the people who were a match could see me.*

She had known this man for years through work but had no idea they had any mutual interest other than they worked in the same building. This is a bonus reason why following your YES is so important. It makes you visible to the people who are a match for you.

Our culture tends to be externally-oriented. We've all heard the advice that if you want to be more magnetic and attract the right people into your life you have to show up differently on the outside. The emphasis is on how you look, where you live, what kind of car you drive, the clothes you wear, and whether you look like the people on screen and in magazines. But if you think about it, when you were a kid in school and they had you rub two pieces of metal together to make a magnet, did you change anything on the outside? No, because what made it magnetic was the alignment inside. This is true for you and me as well. When we're lined up with our truth it automatically magnetizes us and attracts those people, situations and opportunities that match. Jane aligned with her truth by going to the library and look what happened for her.

When you made a magnet as a kid, it only picked up metal. It didn't pick up cloth, or rubber, or wood, only metal. Why? Because that's what it aligned with. The same goes for you. When you follow your YES you create a magnetic field which attracts only those things that are in harmony with your truth.

The windfall is that aligning with your truth and following your YES also makes you uninteresting to the ones who aren't a match for you. You will literally repel the wrong people, circumstances and opportunities you used to attract. You won't have to deal with them anymore.

Be honest with people about who you are, what excites you, your passions and the level of respect required to spend time with you. Honesty and boundaries only intimidate people who aren't a match for you.

Don't trade who you are for who you think the world needs.
Because the world needs you to be you.[6]

- Jay Shetty

Let's revisit our rose analogy. A rose doesn't bloom for you. It blooms because that's who it is. If a rose gets its needs met, it will bloom ... period. There's no alternative. If its needs aren't met, no bloom. But it's here to be a rose and to bloom, and so are you.

We all have strengths, talents, and special knacks for certain things, but when we deny them, or we won't allow ourselves to have the things we know we need to blossom, everybody loses.

If you're walking down the street and there's a rosebush without any blooms on it, you're probably not going to give it much attention. It's not that interesting, right? It's just a thorny green plant.

Let's say you walk down this same street a few weeks later, and now there are some buds on the rosebush. It hasn't bloomed yet, but there are some buds and it's showing promise. What happens? You probably think something like, "I can't wait until it blooms."

A couple weeks later, the blooms are out, and it's breathtaking. You stop and smell the roses. You enjoy this. It's so beautiful. Now you're thinking, "I want to make sure it keeps blooming."

That's what happens when we bloom, we attract the people who want to support us and help us to continue to bloom. And we bloom when we get our needs met by following our YES,

Now, if someone doesn't like roses, they can keep walking until they find the flower they prefer. Whatever aligns for them is perfect.

That's the beauty of life. We don't have to all be roses. We just have to bloom and be ourselves.

When I was 19, I made a shift and decided to be more myself. It made a huge difference even though at first glance it appeared to be no big deal.

My entire life orange has been my favorite color. (Hmmm, perhaps THAT is why I loved the baby aspirin rose so much?!) But as a young child something made me believe having orange as a favorite color was not acceptable.

No one had orange as a favorite color. Blue, red, even green, were totally acceptable as a favorite color. Purple and yellow occasionally were accepted as favorite colors for those outlier kids. But orange? Never.

I'm not sure where I got this idea. I could have been coloring with my brothers and one of them said orange was ugly or no one likes orange. It's possible someone laughed at me for liking orange. I'm not sure where this belief came from, but I knew I had to do something about my misguided color affinity.

Before I started kindergarten, I devised what I thought was a brilliant solution. It was a simple solution really, I just decided to make red my favorite color. I told myself red was close enough and I could make red work.

So for years when asked what my favorite color was I would say red. And every time I did, I could feel the falseness in my answer even though it was readily accepted by the person asking.

As a result of this lie I was telling the world, I received gifts that were red. A red toy truck, a red sweater, a red bicycle. And every time I received one of these red gifts I could feel the disconnect. The disappointment I felt was totally on me. It was like telling someone you wear a large shirt because you are uncomfortable admitting you really wear an extra-large and then they give you a beautiful shirt but it doesn't quite fit.

The person giving me the gift often would say "When we found it in your favorite color we just knew you would love it." This would have been true if red was actually my favorite color, but by misrepresenting my true favorite color, I was setting them up to let me down.

Then one day when I was in college, I decided to own orange as my favorite color. I think it was because I attended a university whose colors were red, white and black and I did not desire to wear any of the school gear. I got tired of all the red everywhere. There was no denying that even though I had told the world red was my favorite color, it was not.

Immediately after I started owning that my favorite color is orange, I started meeting others who loved orange too. Many of them also had been hiding their passion for orange and when I would say my favorite color was orange thy would joyously declare, "Me too!"

I started wearing orange shirts. Often people would say, you don't see a lot of people wearing orange. It really looks good on you. At that point I would proudly declare "Orange is my favorite color." And it never failed that someone in earshot would say, "Me too." By owning orange as my favorite color it made me more visible to the people in my life who were a match for me. Often we would find we had a lot of other things in common. And many times they were people I had found interesting before I knew of our color alignment, but could not figure out why I was drawn to them.

Your YES is what you need to bloom, and you have to own it. Whenever we make someone guess, everyone loses. Nine times out of ten the person who has to guess will guess wrong and feel like a failure, and you will not receive what you need and as a result, not bloom. Owning what you need to bloom means taking responsibility for your needs. A lot of people view responsibilities as burdens, but in reality, they are opportunities. And once you view them as opportunities you get excited about owning your needs.

You've probably heard the saying "the icing on the cake," which simply means something that makes a good situation even better. Example: "I was excited to be promoted and to get a company car too was the icing on the cake." In order for there to be someplace for the icing to go there has to be a cake first, right? Here is where your YES comes in. Your YESES are the ingredients that make up your cake. By following your YES you are making sure all the ingredients for your cake are included in the proper proportions. By doing this you are now prepared. You have baked your cake, so when the icing shows up, in the form of the company car, romantic partner, or all-expenses paid trip, then there is someplace to put it. And the bonus is, in the meantime, you still get to have cake.

Waiting for the "icing" to show up before you bake the cake never works. You'll have missed out on your opportunity.

Luck is what happens when preparation meets opportunity.[7]

- Seneca

Following your YESES is the preparation you do so when opportunity presents itself, you are ready to embrace it. Luck happens when you follow your YES.

The three biggest payoffs of following your YES are:

- **eliminates overwhelm**
- **removes competition**
- **attracts the people, situations and opportunities that match you**

Your YES is a message from Infinite Intelligence
that is pointing you in the direction of your highest good.

— 3 —

What Is Your YES?

Your YES is the thing you know feels right, but you aren't sure why. It's that thing where once you choose it you think, "Yeah, I knew that was the right choice." Or another way you may have encountered your YES is when you "know better" but do it anyway and then you pay the price for not listening to your YES. Perhaps you are very good at being able to carry all the groceries into the house in one trip. Then one day you get in inkling that this time you should take more than one trip, but you ignore it. Sure enough, you end up dropping the bag with the eggs in it or smashing the bread. Your YES is a thing you know to be true, but you don't know how you know it. Some people call it your intuition.

You must train your intuition — you must trust the small voice inside you which tells you exactly what to say, what to decide.

- Ingrid Bergman[8]

There are a great many different words for your YES: intuition, truth, calling, passion, soul, gut, essence, even your life force. Quite simply, your YES is a message from Infinite Intelligence that is pointing you in the direction of your highest good. It's a lighthouse illuminating the way no matter how dark it may get.

More times than not your YES is a rather mundane thing, instead of an earth-shattering, life-changing epiphany. Those seemingly humdrum YESES make up the majority of our lives. Like when you feel inspired to take a different route home from work and find out later there was a big accident on your normal route which had backed up traffic for hours. Or when for some reason you pass on the ice cream being offered at your friend's dinner party, even though you love ice cream, and the next day everyone who was at the dinner party, except you, is ill with salmonella poisoning because the ice cream had been contaminated. (This actually happened to me.)

As you read this book you are likely to find yourself recalling instances from your past where your YES presented itself. Perhaps for you it was the YES that led you to take a certain vacation, purchase the car you now drive, or choose to wear the shoes you have on. Whether you followed these YESES or not is not important right now. Simply allow yourself to start to recognize how often you encounter YESES in your life.

INSIDER TIP:

Your YES is the thing that feels the most supportive of you being your best in this moment.

The question you want to ask yourself is, "What do I need to be my best right now?"

This is not, "What do I need to be my best forever?" Nor is it, "What do I need to be the best I can ever be," and it certainly is not, "What do I need to be the best anyone's ever been?"

Simply: what do you need to support yourself in being the best you can be here in this moment?

Let me share an everyday, run-of-the-mill kind of YES I encountered.

In my early 20s, fresh out of college, as I walked through a bookstore a copy of *Peter the Great* caught my eye. I wasn't sure why, I hadn't studied Russian history and only vaguely knew who Peter the Great was, but for some reason I felt compelled to make this book my own. As I went to pick it up out of the stacks of books on the table, I was surprised how much more difficult it was to lift up than I expected. Turned out, the book was huge — nearly three inches thick and over 1800 pages long. It was more than three times the size of any book I had ever read in my life. That would have been enough to deter me in the past, but for some reason not this time. My brain was saying, "Are you nuts? This book is huge. It's like reading a dictionary where half the words in it are in Russian. You'll never finish this. You're wasting your money."

On top of all the things my brain was telling me, I was not a spontaneous shopper by nature. I tended to put a lot of thought into a purchase, and yet I bought it anyway.

I had no idea where this purchase or the book would lead. I didn't even know if I could read such a big and challenging book, but I knew it was my YES. Even though it was full of very difficult to pronounce Russian names and places, it is still one of my favorite books of all time. I loved it, but it did not lead me to becoming a Russian history junkie, instead it was a gateway to me no longer being intimidated by the size of a book.

You can think of the way your YESES come together to make up your life much like constructing a brick building. There are a few big cornerstone YESES which make up your foundation, like where you live, what you do with your life, who you share your life with and so on, but the majority of the YESES you will encounter are just regular old bricks. They are pretty similar in size with thousands of them coming together to make up the majority of the structure.

To give you an idea of a how a YES impacted my life path on a grander scale, this is actually one of my cornerstone YESES, check this out:

In July of 1996 I was living in Peoria, Illinois working my tail off starting a business. All week I was in sales meetings and marketing presentations and on the weekends I was driving all over the Mid-west attending trainings. Then I'd drive back home late Sunday night and start all over again Monday morning. Twelve- to fifteen-hour days, seven days a week.

It was exciting, but I was wearing out. Not enough sleep, too much fast food, and not taking any time to relax and recharge. I needed a break.

A couple of guys I had met at some trainings had recently moved to Boulder, Colorado to open an office and I went for a visit. I don't remember much about the week I was there other than I would wake up every morning look out the window and say out loud, "Another beautiful day in the Magic Kingdom." (I interned at Disney World while I was in college.) I couldn't get over how beautiful it was there. Next thing I knew I was looking in the paper to find a place to live. Something deep down inside told me this was home.

Without making any formal declarations, I knew by the time I drove back to Peoria, I would be moving to Colorado. As I drove through town, I passed an apartment complex where my friend Shelly shared a place with her twin sister. Her sister was getting married soon and I remember thinking I didn't even know if Shelly still lived there or not. The thought passed and I drove on. Less than fifteen minutes after I walked in my door the phone rang. It was Shelly. She said her sister was getting married that coming weekend and she was going to move at the end of the month and wondered if I would tell her who I worked with to find my place because she really liked it.

Without a moment of hesitation I said, "Do you want to sub-let my place? Because I'm moving to Colorado ... ."

Wait, did I just say that? Shelly was thrilled and said she would take it.

Without ever telling anyone of my intention to move, I had sublet my place in only a couple of minutes. Our conversation continued and Shelly said she was going to need some new things like a bed, a dining room table and chairs, a couch and a TV. Those were the same things I knew I was not taking with me when I moved, and we agreed she would purchase all of them from me when she came to sign the lease.

Bam!

In less than fifteen minutes I had my place rented, all the furnishings I wanted to sell were sold and I had yet to tell anyone but Shelly that I was moving.

Every YES leads to another, but you have to do the first one to get to the next.

(You're going to read this a lot in this book because knowing every YES you follow leads to another YES will keep you going when you can't comprehend how the YES you just responded to will serve you.)

And the magic of following my YES didn't end there. When I arrived in Boulder a month later I had no place to go. I hadn't really thought this all through. I was staying with the guys I visited earlier but I had no home of my own and was starting all over with my business. I was definitely going to have to keep following my YESES.

My next YES was to walk downtown in order to find a place to live. I hit the street thinking I was either going to walk by a great apartment complex or find a real estate office to help me find one.

Then I heard a woman's voice shout, "Hey Ken!"

Since I had only been in town a few hours and knew no women in Boulder, I assumed she was not addressing me, so I didn't look to see who it was.

Then again, "Ken!"

I'm thinking, who is that woman yelling at?

Finally, she yelled, "KEN BECHTEL!"

I turned around and saw Marcia, a girl I had gone to summer camp with back in Illinois when I was a kid. Turns out she was getting her Master's degree at the University of Colorado in Boulder and spotted me from across the street. We chatted for a while and I told her I had just arrived in town.

She invited me to join her and a group of friends for dinner that night at a local brew pub. It just so happened one of Marcia's friends in her grad program was looking to fill her place in a great house on "The Hill." She told me all about it, and before the evening was over I had a place to live.

Only then did I understand what my YES to "take a walk downtown to find a place to live" was all about.

Your YES only reveals the next step to you. Never more. Each step is only revealed after you have taken the preceding one. You have to trust and take action.

In the movie *Indiana Jones and the Last Crusade* there is a scene where Indiana Jones (Harrison Ford) is following the notes in a diary to find the Holy Grail. The last challenge he must overcome is finding the hidden bridge over a bottomless pit.

You may recall watching Indie stand at the edge of a sheer cliff looking down into a bottomless crevasse, then over to the cliff on the other side and saying, "Impossible. Nobody can jump this."

Then he hears his father, played by Sean Connery, moaning as he lay dying and Indie realizes that in order to get across this bottomless pit safely he needs to take a leap of faith, and he doesn't look too excited about it.

Next you hear his father say, "You must believe, boy. You must believe."

Then Indie puts his hand over his heart, closes his eyes, takes a deep breath and you can literally see him getting out of his head, his thoughts and his fears, and into his heart. A few more deep breaths and then he does it. He takes a leap of faith by trusting that by taking this step he will be supported and sure enough the hidden bridge across the bottomless pit is there to support him. That first step of following his YES revealed his next step/YES.

Big or small, scary or comfortable, your YES is always leading you to more YESES and your highest good. Take a leap of faith, trust and proceed.

One other thing to be aware of regarding your YESES is that there is one YES you are acting on directly in this moment, but it does not mean there is only one YES in action. There are many layers.

For instance, I had the YES to write this book, which is a bigger, more long-term YES. Within the YES of writing this book there are shorter-term YESES like what do I work on next, such as the layout or a certain chapter revision or even to step away and not do anything on the book right now.

There are multiple layers of YESES in action at any one time. Your job is to focus on the one that's most pertinent in this moment.

Quite frequently the YES which is most pertinent in the moment is playing a role in a more long-term YES.

If building a skyscraper is your long-term YES, in this moment your YES may be to pour the foundation, add another layer of bricks, or install the windows. All of which come together to as part of the skyscraper. Do you see it?

Following your YES is speaking, acting upon, and living your truth now, with no attachment, agenda, or required response. Simply expressing your truth in the moment for no other reason than because it is your truth and you need to express it through words or actions without first filtering it through if someone else will like it or trying to control how they will react. This is why your YES feels so freeing.

Are you starting to recall some times when you followed your YES and it led to more YESES for you? If so, grab a note pad and write them down as you remember them. Allow these memories to be reminders of how capable you already are at following your YES. If you're not recalling any times when you followed your YES yet, don't worry, I promise you will soon. Everyone has followed their YES before, but you may not have thought of it in these terms.

INSIDER TIP:

Your YES is generous. Even though the question I encourage you to ask to connect with your YES is "What do I need to be my best right now?" What you need is not always something you get or receive. If all I got from that huge book on Peter the Great was my all-time favorite door stop, it would have been fine. It could be that you need to pass on a front row parking spot so someone else can have it and you can get some extra exercise by walking a little farther. It could be you need to invite someone to join you on a project so you can train them to enhance their career.

Your YES is just as likely to be about giving and being generous as it is about receiving and being grateful. Be sure to look for both aspects when you look for yours.

Your YES is a feeling that invites
you forward and inspires you to act.

— 4 —

Finding Your YES

"Where do I find my YES?"

This is one of the most common questions I receive. Everyone wants to know where to go looking for their YES, and how do they know it's **their** YES when they find it?

It may surprise you to learn that your YES is already within you. Every moment of your life your YES is right there with you if you'll pay attention to it.

There are different ways to be aware of your YES. Some people feel it viscerally, others hear it, and some sense it energetically, more of a knowingness - that's me. Know that there is no one "right" way. Whatever feels best to you, go with it.

One of the first things you must do to recognize your YES is to be present, open and receptive to it. This means you let go of knowing how or when or why it will show up and simply stay open to the possibility of divine guidance coming to you anytime, anyplace, any way.

Reverend Michael Beckwith[9] says it this way:

Some people say God spoke to me today ... I say, no, you listened.

You may be trying to figure out where your treasure trove of YESES is located. Getting all up in your head and overthinking this will be a barrier to recognizing your YES.

We often think of yes and no as intellectual choices. "Yes, I want to do this." or "No, I don't want to do that." "Yes, you're right." or "No, you're not right." Intellectual yeses and nos definitely exist. Like the traffic light is red, so no don't proceed. Or the traffic light turned green so yes it's safe to go. But that is different than your YES.

What we're talking about here with your YES, is the *feeling* of YES.

I know you've had times when something just "felt right." Sometimes we express it as "It felt like the thing to do." Perhaps you were lost driving in an area that was new to you and even though your head was telling you to keep going straight you had a feeling you needed to turn right and following the feeling led you to where you needed to be. We've all had experiences like this. Notice these are feelings.

The feeling of YES is your divine guidance.

The Divine communicates with us through feelings, not through ideas, words or data. The language of the Divine is feelings. So, following your YES is committing to paying attention to, listening to, and following your feelings of YES.

To find your YES you must feel it out. It lives in your heart. Your YES is a feeling that invites you forward and inspires you to act.

Following your YES is not so much a decision-making process as it is a direction-finding process: identifying the direction of your next step in your heart, and then deciding to move in that direction in whatever way is available to you in this moment. Following your YES is about the direction you are taking with your life via the choices and actions you take each day.

I encourage you to stop using your brain to try and figure out what your heart wants. Instead of trying to figure it out, feel it out.

"It's impossible" said pride.
"It's risky" said experience.
"It's pointless" said reason.
"Give it a try" whispered the heart.

- Unknown

No matter how much of a thinker or brain-centered person you think you are you can still connect with your heart and your YES. Prior to becoming a world renowned energy healer, my good friend Jeffrey Allen[10] spent lots of time in his head as an engineer and mathematician. Here's how he puts it:

> *"As much as I like, using my mind, it's not a good tool for making decisions.*
>
> *I like to say, 'I'm gonna have to make a decision before I think about anything.' Because if I think about it, I get really confused. I get all these ideas. And I imagine all these possibilities and outcomes and stuff. But I don't need that.*
>
> *I made a commitment to myself. I'm simply gonna follow my YESES and see what happens. Because, it makes life interesting."*

You might be in your head right now trying to understand what you just read; trying to figure out how it fits in your life.

INSIDER TIP:

Take a minute right now and use this simple technique to get out of your head and into your heart so you can connect with your YES as it shows up as the feeling that it is.

When you notice you are in your head trying to figure things out (for me I will literally catch myself looking up as if I can look into my head and see the answer), pause, tip your head forward, look directly at your heart, take a deep relaxing breath and ask, "How do I feel about this right now?"

Trust the answer you get. It doesn't have to make sense. In fact, it likely won't make sense. Feelings are not rational or logical, but they are unarguable.

When I was a young boy I was scared of the dark. On our farm we had a detached garage, which meant we had to walk about 100 feet in the dark to get to our house whenever we got home at night.

I was so afraid of the dark that I would run as fast as I could from the garage to the house. I tried to cover my fear by saying it was a race with my brothers to see who could get to the house first, but I'm not sure I fooled anyone.

This feeling didn't make sense. There was no logic to it. After all, no one else in my family was afraid of the dark, so why was I?

None of that intellectual stuff mattered. I can tell you even though I couldn't rationalize why I was scared of the dark, that feeling was very real.

Of course the answer you get when you ask yourself, "How do I feel about this?" could be any feeling: joy, excitement, curiosity, peace, nervousness, concern, fear etc. Be open and trust whatever feeling shows up, this is your divine guidance.

Sadly many of us have cut ourselves off from our heart and our feelings because at some point in our lives we had some bad experiences or got our feelings hurt, and so we started building walls to protect ourselves. When we did this, we also cut ourselves off from our YESES.

A few years ago, this thought came to me: "When you separate from your heart, you die a little."

I had actively separated from my heart so many times, I was practically dead. Sure, I was breathing and all, but I'm talking about being emotionally dead. I had been separating from my heart as my means of coping for a very long time, and I'm pretty sure I am not alone in this habit. I have no doubt this all started for me as a way of "being strong" during the long series of funerals I attended growing up.

When I was 21-years-old my father died, and by that time I had already attended funerals for twenty members of my family. I literally spent a big chunk of my childhood attending funerals for grandparents, aunts, uncles, cousins, a classmate and eventually my Dad.

I learned at a very young age how to suppress my feelings and not cry from all the trips with my parents to visit family member's bedsides in retirement homes, then in hospital rooms after they had a stroke or a heart attack, and ultimately while attending their visitations and funerals. Through all of this I never saw my Dad cry, and I pretty much always wanted to do everything like my Dad, so I didn't cry either.

In fact, when I was a young boy it was a running joke in my family that I would follow his lead no matter what. If Dad had a second helping of potatoes, I had more potatoes too. If Dad wore a coat when he left the house, you had better believe I did as well.

I got so good at suppressing my feelings that I didn't cry no matter whose funeral it was or how well I knew them.

I remember being 10-years-old at my paternal grandmother's funeral. After the service I walked up to my Dad and pulled on his sleeve as I proudly said in my high-pitched 10-year-old voice, "I didn't cry Dad. I didn't cry." He turned around with tears in his eyes and said, in his big grown-up man voice, "That's good son."

It felt like I had just betrayed him. I didn't understand it. I just knew I desperately wanted to cry then to be in support of him in some way, but I couldn't. I had separated from my heart and locked down my ability to cry so tightly, I couldn't squeeze out a tear even when I wanted to.

Not long after my conversation with Kurt, my friend who first said everything is either a YES or a NO, where we talked about living life by going from YES to YES to YES, I realized if I wanted to embrace this way of life I'd need to figure out how to reconnect with my heart, tear down the walls I had built around it, take off the armor, and let my heart have room to feel again.

Now whenever I feel myself closing off, I take a deep breath, tip my head forward and look directly at my heart and feel into the guidance there to support me in being me and being happy.

Your YES is loving and supportive.
It is not there to judge you.

Michael Neill[11], author of *The Inside-Out Revolution*, explains exactly how to identify your YES:

How can you tell the inner voice from all of the other voices in your head? The inner voice is the one that doesn't think you suck.

Another thing which will help you identify your YES is to know it's never drawing you *away* from something, it is always nudging you *towards* something. Here's what I mean:

I have a morning routine of waking up, using the bathroom, making my bed, drinking a glass of water, doing a series of body stretches, meditating, exercising, taking a shower and then reading with a cup of chai. Even though this is my routine, I still check in every day to see if it's my YES that day. At least 95% of the time it is, but on occasion I will be guided to skip the stretches or the exercise or meditate later. It's not a matter of resisting whatever is the thing I'm guided not to do that day, like "I don't want to have to exercise today." The reason my routine shifts every once in a while, is because something else is my YES in that moment.

Perhaps I'm really excited to dive into a project for work, or I want to spend more time reading, and so I postpone the exercise. Sometimes I have something else going on later in the day which will provide exercise so I can do a different activity in the morning. In all these cases, I am following my YES and moving towards whatever in the moment supports me in being my best.

Your YES is never resistance to what you *don't* want. It's always identifying what aligns most precisely for you to be your best right now.

We are all human and you are going to catch yourself some days goin', "Man, that takes a lot of time. I don't really want to have to do all that stretching today." That's resistance. When you notice you are in resistance, flip it around and ask, "What supports me in being my best right now?"

Your YES is always about what will contribute to you blooming. It's never about avoiding something that doesn't. It's not, "I don't want to eat Italian or Mexican or Greek food." It's, "I want ice cream." Also be aware your YES is never in regard to someone else.

For example it is never regarding:

- Your spouse/boyfriend/girlfriend doing something different.
- Your children behaving differently.
- Your client or your boss treating you differently.

Your YES is always regarding you.

Sure, it may impact or affect other people. It may include other people, too but it's not about them.

Another thing to be aware of is we often want our YES to be some kind of big obvious "holy-cow" communication.

For example the time my friend Tom Davis had driven 300 miles from his home in Chapel Hill, N.C. to visit me in Washington, D.C. We went to lunch and he looked at the menu for no more than 5 seconds, closed it and declared, "I know what I'm having!"

Surprised, I asked how he made such a quick decision. He opened his menu and showed me there was a Tom Davis Burger on the menu. No kidding! He didn't even read what was on the burger. He just knew it was his YES.

As Tom said, "When a restaurant you've never been to before literally has a meal with your name on it you have to order it."

This kind of super obvious YES does happen from time to time, like it did for Tom, however the truth is your YES can be, and more often than not *is* subtle. We have to tune ourselves in to subtleties. You develop your ability to recognize the subtleties of our YES much in the same way we develop our palate.

Let's use wine as an example: To a beginner the wine either tastes good or bad. This is a fine place to start. Over time, as the wine drinker gains more experience with wine, they learn to appreciate the distinct flavors. Their palate becomes more refined and they notice subtle distinctions between different wines. Now instead of saying the wine tastes good or bad they might say, "This wine is surprisingly earthy and tannic, considering how fruit forward yet buttery it is." (Clearly I'm not a wine expert. Those terms probably don't even go together. Full disclosure, I cobbled them together from something I found online.)

The point is we develop our awareness to the subtleties of our YES over time too.

It takes time and practice. The process can be fun, much like tasting wine can be fun, if we let it. The key to having it be fun is to let yourself be a beginner.

I've been following my YES for years and I still consider myself a beginner ... it takes the pressure off.

Now that you are aware your YES can be subtle and that it resides in your heart, you are miles ahead of where I was when I started. I was used to looking in my head for big obvious holy-cow YESES. I wasted so much time trying to figure them out, instead of feeling them out. I assure you that disregarding all my more subtle YESES delayed my progress, but I'm dialed in now. When you follow these practices, you too will be dialed in very soon.

Your YES is a beacon out in front of
you which is calling you forward.

— 5 —

Trust Your YES

When you feel that feeling, that guidance, your YES ... trust it, because it is your truth. It is your life force striving to express itself in the world. Trust is a muscle we all must develop if we want our life to be more fluid, relaxed and fulfilling.

In the Spring of 2010 I trusted a YES and started a radio show even though I knew nothing about producing, creating or broadcasting on radio. At first, I thought it was a crazy idea. How could I possibly pull this off with such limited knowledge of how radio worked. I considered taking some courses to learn more before I started, but then I realized this was just a delay tactic my brain was employing to keep me from doing something new. I just needed to do my part, be the host, and trust that being the producer or engineer of the show was someone else's YES. Ultimately, it didn't feel risky because I stayed aligned with my truth of hosting a show.

People would tell me how courageous I was to take such a big risk, but to me it was the most natural thing in the world.

One way to recognize your YES is often things seem to magically lineup.

They often feel effortless. All you must do is trust and step into them.

When I first got the idea for my radio show, I contacted my friend Chelsea who is a graphic designer about creating a logo for me. I didn't really know exactly what I wanted, but I gave her the name I had for the show - Finding You in the Goo, and some general ideas.

When we got back together not only was the logo exactly what had come to me after our meeting, it was also the exact colors I had envisioned. Because it was my YES it flowed with ease and there was no doubt I had found my logo and my graphic designer.

It doesn't always happen on the first try, but when you follow your YES you don't compromise. Your YES is a beacon out in front of you which is calling you forward.

Back in the Spring of 2003, I was on a hike outside of Boulder when I stopped at one of my favorite overlooks to enjoy the view. As I sat there I wondered, "If I could do anything right now, what would I want to do?"

The answer I received was: learn about building straw bale houses. I had read about them and done a couple of workshops on the subject, but I wanted full immersion. I wanted to really learn all about it, and specifically about natural plastering. This had been an interest of mine for years.

Kind of funky, not real practical, but it was something I always was interested in and wanted to learn more about. This was exciting to me, and I liked where this was heading.

The very next thought I had was, why would I do that? Am I going to become a professional straw bale house builder? Is there even a need for such a thing? Do I really think I have the ability to make it a career?

This is a great demonstration of what Academy Award winning actor Rex Harrison[12] meant when he said -

Exhilaration is that feeling you get just after a great idea hits you, and just before you realize what's wrong with it.

Our brains are wired for survival and therefore the unfamiliar feels unsafe to our brains. This chatter in my head was my brain trying to talk me out of doing something unfamiliar/unsafe which it was not sure I could survive.

When I got home I amazingly located an email I had received several months prior from a man in Wisconsin who was building a straw bale house and looking for an apprentice. In the email he explained how he had years of experience in this kind of building, he would provide a spare room in his family's home and provide all meals, and I would get to work with him and learn all about building a straw bale house and natural plastering.

I contacted him, it sounded like a good match and we agreed I would start at the end of the month. I moved out of my rental home in Colorado, put all my worldly possessions in my friend's garage, so the only bills I had were my cell phone and gas for my car, and drove to Mount Horeb, Wisconsin, famous for Norwegian trolls and home of the Mount Horeb Mustard Museum. (I kid you not.)

I get there and a few weeks in, it is clear this is not the place for me. There was no apprenticeship, this guy was just looking for cheap help. The owner/builder was not even showing up at job site. I wasn't learning anything, just doing manual labor.

I asked myself what would support me in being my best self right now, and my YES was I needed to terminate this agreement.

The night after I notified him I would be moving on in two weeks, I was pretty down. I'd been so excited about this opportunity to learn the art of building a straw bale house hands on and now it all seemed to be unraveling. The thought of going back home without fulfilling this desire was depressing. Yet, something told me my YES was on point. It was just the form I thought this YES was supposed to take was a bit off. I was sure there was more, and my YES had not been wrong. Before I knew it, through what many would call miraculous happenings, I found two other options that were even better opportunities.

I had met a woman named Amy at a straw bale workshop in Tucson, Arizona the previous winter who told me she and her partner Brian were going to be building a straw bale house on their property in upstate New York that summer. I decided to contact her to see if I could continue learning while helping on their house. Now this was back in the early 2000s not everyone had cell phones, most people still had land lines, plus email was not nearly as common as it is now. I did not have an email for Amy and the phone number I had for her was a Pennsylvania number so I knew it might not find her there, but what did I have to lose? The phone went to voicemail and the message was one of those generic, "The person at xxx-xxx-xxxx is unable to take your call ..." things so I didn't even find out if this was still Amy's number or not. My YES to continue my adventure in learning this building technique was so compelling I was open to all possibilities, even the long-shots. And since this was the only way I had to contact her, I left a message with my new cellphone number hoping it would reach her and she'd call back.

When I didn't hear back from Amy I wondered if Vonda, another woman I'd met in the Tucson workshop would know how to contact Amy in New York. All I had was an email for Vonda, so I sent her a note telling her about my situation and asking if she knew how to get a hold of Amy. Vonda replied right away. The only contact she had for Amy was the Pennsylvania phone number. No help there. Then she noted that she and her husband were doing a bunch of natural plastering in the house they were remodeling and if I wanted to come out and help them in late August they would be happy to take care of my room and board.

This sounded promising, but it was only mid-June and I was leaving the project in Wisconsin at the end of the month. What was I going to do in the meantime? I still had my YES of learning about straw bale. I had followed my YES to contact Amy, but it had been a dead end. There was a possible option in California in a couple of months, but in the moment I felt like I had come to the end of the road. That is, until ...

A couple days later the family I was "apprenticing" with in Wisconsin said I had received a letter in the mail. This surprised me as I had not forwarded my mail from Colorado and other than my family, no one had the address in Wisconsin. Naturally I assumed it must be from someone in my family, but it wasn't ... it was from Amy.

To this day I have no idea how this letter got to me. All my mail was being held, and I had not thought to leave my mailing address on the voicemail message, but somehow Amy's letter had reached me. Something magical was happening.

I opened the letter and couldn't believe what I read. It was as if Amy was replying to all the questions that had been rolling around in my head. She wrote that she and Brian were indeed building their straw bale house. She went on to mention starting in mid-July Paul Lacinski would be helping them with plastering the house and invited me to come out.

I about fell over. Paul Lacinski was the guy who wrote the book - *Serious Straw Bale*[13] - that was practically the Bible of straw bale building at the time. My YES had just taken me from what I thought was a dead end in Wisconsin, where the builder/homeowner was trying to figure out how to build his home using Home Depot DIY books, to working hands-on with the big Kahuna of the straw bale world. And the timing was perfect. Plus, there was ten days between when I wrapped things up in Wisconsin and when I needed to be in New York. So, I drove down to visit my family in Illinois over the 4th of July week, an unexpected bonus.

By following my YES to terminate what I had thought was going to be a dream apprentice situation in Wisconsin, without giving up on my YES to work on straw bale houses and learn natural plastering, I ended up with two much more advantageous options. I chose both. My journey ended up extending for eight months, continuing from Wisconsin to upstate New York, to Santa Barbara, California and back to Colorado.

In return for my labor, they provided room and board and I received the best real-world education on straw bale building and natural plastering imaginable. I have to tell you, by following my YES I felt more fulfilled and abundant during that time period than ever before in my life. Everything flowed. I felt appreciated. I felt like I was contributing. I felt confident. I felt excited. I felt respected and I trusted what was showing up. Timing lined up. Opportunities lined up, and I just kept asking myself "What is my YES in this moment?" and trusting.

The more you trust your intuition, the more empowered you become, the stronger you become, and the happier you become.

- Gisele Bundchen[14]

As a result of trusting the Universe and following my YES again and again I had the experience of a lifetime. I met some of the most amazing people, and traveled across the country while having my expenses covered.

When I decided to follow my YES as I sat on the hillside during my hike, I thought it would lead to me working in the straw bale construction field upon my return. It didn't. It took me in another direction entirely, but that's a story for another time.

The point is you don't have to know where your YES will ultimately lead you before you follow it. It's normal to think you know, like I did, but chances are you will be surprised by where you end up. Trust and follow it anyway and you can have amazing adventures fill your life.

— 6 —

Who Benefits by You Following Your YES?

Following your YES so you can be your best is a gift to everyone.

Think about it, do your coworkers and your customers benefit when you are being your best in your work? Does your romantic partner benefit when you are being your best in your interactions with them? Do your kids (if you have them) benefit when you are showing up as your best self? And how about your family members, do they benefit?

No one has ever expressed this as beautifully as Marianne Williamson did in her extraordinary poem entitled "Our Deepest Fear":

Our deepest fear is not that we are inadequate.
Our deepest fear is that we are powerful beyond measure.
It is our light, not our darkness
That most frightens us.

We ask ourselves
Who am I to be brilliant, gorgeous, talented, fabulous?
Actually, who are you not *to be?*
You are a child of God.

Your playing small
Does not serve the world.
There's nothing enlightened about shrinking
So that other people won't feel insecure around you.

We are all meant to shine,
As children do.
We were born to make manifest
The glory of God that is within us.

It's not just in some of us;
It's in everyone.

And as we let our own light shine,
We unconsciously give other people permission to do the same.
As we're liberated from our own fear,
Our presence automatically liberates others.[15]

The first time I read this poem 25 years ago the recognition that I was the person Marianne had written about, who feared my light, brought me to tears.

No one wins when you play small and suppress your own life because you think somebody else cannot handle it. What a selfish way to live. How arrogant to believe we know what someone else can handle. Have you not faced challenges yourself and grown and learned from them? Isn't it selfish to steal that opportunity from another? There is nothing noble about living a diminished or deferred life, waiting for the proverbial "one day" that we all know never comes. I'm not proud of it, but I'm guilty of doing all of this.

I remember standing on the stage singing in a little studio where I was taking a voice class in my early 40s. Half dozen classmates, our instructor Sarah, the accompanist Mike and a special guest instructor Divy were there that day.

When I finished singing Divy said, "That was easy for you, wasn't it?"

I kind of sheepishly admitted it was.

She said, "What keeps you from giving it more?"

I said, "This is going to sound kind of arrogant, but I'm afraid you wouldn't be able to handle it. I don't really know what "it" is, but I have this feeling "it" is too much for anyone."

This was voice class. This was one of the safest environments I had ever been in. We were all there to grow and open up and bring more of ourselves to each song we sang. In fact, one of my classmates, Carol, used to say to me almost every time I finished a song, "That was good, but I wonder what the real Ken Bechtel sounds like."

A few weeks later I had a private lesson with Sarah. We spent the entire hour working on one song, "Iris" by the Goo Goo Dolls[16]. There are two lines repeated throughout the song that go:

And I don't want the world to see me/
'Cause I don't think that they'd understand

I must have sung those lines at least fifty times during my lesson. When our group class started Sarah suggested I sing first since I was already warmed up. When I performed "Iris" this time I didn't hold back at all. As the last note faded Mike, the accompanist said, "Wow!" Carol, with a huge smile of satisfaction on her face said, "So that's what the real Ken Bechtel sounds like!"

And no one was dead.

Turns out they *could* handle "it." There was nothing to be afraid of. The light inside of me wasn't as dangerous as I thought.

Marianne Williamson was right. We, ourselves, are usually the ones most in fear of our greatness. Everyone else is excitedly waiting for it to come out, so let it shine!

No is . . .

You may recall the way my friend Kurt first said this to me was: "It's either YES or it's NO." Which means everything that is not a clear YES is a NO. Something being a NO does not make that thing, person or situation bad, valueless or dangerous. It is just not your YES right now. Just like all the things on a menu that you don't order for lunch are not bad, they just aren't what aligns with you right now.

Notice I am capitalizing NO because it too is guidance from the Divine.

A NO can be a black hole of effort if we are fighting against the fact that it is a NO *right now*. Let your NO be a NO *in this moment* and recognize that if it is meant to be a YES it will show up as a clear YES at the right time.

If you are investing tons of energy and effort with little progress, consider it confirmation that what you are struggling with is a NO right now, no matter how much you want it to be a YES.

I often say that NO is the new YES. Let me be crystal clear - NO is the new YES - does not mean when someone is saying "no" they really mean yes and to disregard their "no" as a smoke screen. It's important to always respect another person's NO or their YES, just as we want ours to be respected. What I mean here is when you say no to someone else you are saying yes to yourself.

It is common for our YES, our internal guidance, to show up as a "NO, don't do that or NO don't go there" or "NO don't eat that." This NO message is your truth. It is your guidance from the Infinite Intelligence.

Author and educator Preston Smiles[17] shares a perfect illustration of what I mean in this story where he followed his YES when it showed up as a NO.

> *When I was 15-years-old, I was in somewhat of a gang. I was on my way out of it, but I was still hanging with some pretty amazing but misguided young men, like myself.*

I got a call one day from one of my best friends, Scott. And he asked me to come out and hang and drink and do these run outs that they used to do. Which is where they would go in a liquor store, grab all the alcohol and run out.

This particular night, it was a no for me.

It was my first understanding of intuition. I didn't really get it. I was fifteen so I didn't have the vocabulary or anything of that nature but something inside of me. Something deep within me said don't go.

So I told Scott, "No man I'm gonna chill."

Scott is like "Oh, you gonna be a (beep)!"

And I said, "Yeah, I'm gonna be a (beep) tonight."

Scott said, "Alright "P" I'll get up with you tomorrow." And hung up the phone.

Within an hour, every single person that was in that blue Astro van that I was in every other night ... was shot.

And my best friend, Scott, was shot in the head and died.

Following my "YES when it showed up as a "No don't go" potentially saved my life.

This is the internal guidance system, that still small voice that's always, in all ways speaking.

If prayer is when we speak to God,
then intuition is when God speaks to us.

\- Wayne Dyer[18]

A “No” uttered from the deepest conviction
is better than a “Yes” merely uttered
to please, or worse, to avoid trouble.

- Gandhi[19]

— 7 —

Do You Love Yourself Enough to Say NO?

People tell me all the time that they are uncomfortable saying "no."

If there is any way they can avoid saying "no" that's what they'll do. They feel saying "no" will create conflict, cause a rift or create separation in some way, and they want to avoid this at all costs. But the truth is there is no way to avoid saying "no." You either say "no" to the other person/opportunity or "no" to yourself. Either way you are saying "no", but do you really enjoy it when you say "no" to yourself?

Let's say a friend who loves horror movies calls you and asks you to go to a new horror movie with them. You don't really want to go because you don't like horror movies. They scare the bejesus out of you and you can't sleep for days after watching one, but you haven't done anything with this friend in a while so you feel obligated and you agree to go. You regretfully sit through the movie with your eyes closed half the time. All the while wishing you had summoned the guts to tell your friend you didn't want to go to this movie with them so you could be doing something you enjoyed right now. The movie ends and your friend says, "You didn't like it did you?" You're stunned. How did they know?

Easy. Your body language, your energy and your lack of involvement is like a great big "Hated it!" sign on your forehead. Now not only do you feel like you wasted your time, your friend feels guilty for dragging you to a film you did not enjoy.

The reality is this experience is not the result of you not having enough guts to say no to your friend. It is the result of you not having enough appreciation for yourself to follow your YES and say yes to you.

If it's not growing you, supporting you, educating you,
or inspiring you . . . it is not FOR you!

- Jennifer Price[20]

I ran across this question in a meme recently and I think it is interesting to consider as we address this topic —

If I asked you to name all the things you love, how long would it take for you to name yourself? Most people tell me they didn't even think to include themselves on this list.

Do you love yourself enough to say "no" to another in order to be true to yourself?

Did you realize every time you say yes to something that does not align or resonate with your truth you are saying no to yourself?

We really have 3 options in life:

1. You agree to do something that doesn't align with your truth – say yes to them and no to yourself.
2. You decide not to do a thing that doesn't align with your truth – say no to them and yes to yourself.
3. You agree to do something that does align with your truth – say yes to you and to them, there-by saying no to other options.

Do you see how we always say "no" to someone or something? I encourage you to let go of the myth that there is a way to avoid saying "no." It is amazing how much easier it is for most people to say no to themselves than it is to say no to someone else. Where's the love for yourself in that? How many times have you been out to eat at a restaurant and the food you were served was unsatisfactory in some way? The entree was not prepared to your liking. The salad dressing was on your salad when you had requested it on the side. Or something else was not as you had requested it.

When the wait staff came by and asked, what I think is the broadest question one can ask, "How is everything?" Did you let them know you were displeased, or did you smile and say "really good" or "great" or "excellent?"

Here is a situation where the person whose job it is to ensure you enjoy your food asks you to help them make sure you have a good dining experience and you say, "no I will not accept your offer of assistance," and lie to them about your meal in order to avoid saying no. But you still said no. You just said it to yourself. Do you see it?

Following your YES is about loving yourself so you can bring the best version of yourself to everyone you meet and every situation you encounter. Love yourself enough to say no and everyone benefits.

All the mistakes I ever made were when
I wanted to say 'no' and said 'yes.'

- Moss Hart[21]

Your awareness of what you don’t want
is the invitation to explore what you do want.

— 8 —

YDKWYWUYKWYDW

This stands for: You Don't Know What You Want Until You Know What You Don't Want.

Knowing what you don't want is not a dead end. It's the start. We tend to want to say I just don't want this or that and stop there, but this doesn't get you any closer to your goal. We're used to focusing on the thing we don't want and then going into "protect ourself" mode. We get so stuck on the NO part and put all our energy into avoiding this thing we don't want, when the more empowering approach is to repurpose that energy into creating what we do want.

Rather than focusing on problems, focus inventively, intentionally on what solutions might look or feel like. Our mind is meant to generate ideas that help us escape circumstantial traps - if we trust it to do so.

- Marsha Sinetar[22]

Your awareness of what you don't want is the invitation to explore what you do want. The NOs you receive in life are very good things. They refine your aim and help you zero in on what serves you in being your best.

Don't be afraid of NO; it is actually your friend.

If you are reading this book and beating yourself up because you're great at identifying your NOs, but feel like you have no idea what your YES is and therefore, asking yourself, how will I ever be able to follow my YES if I can't find it, know this: Your NO is telling you to look somewhere other than this NO for what will support you in being your best. It is not telling you there is no support available for you. Often you must experience one or more NOs to get clarity on your YES.

If you recall my journey to learn about building straw bale houses, my experience in Wisconsin was clearly a NO, but the experience clarified my YES of how important to me it was to learn about this subject. However, the form of learning available to me in Wisconsin was not in alignment for me.

When you're putting together a jigsaw puzzle and you try to place a piece but it doesn't fit, that's a NO. It's not good. It's not bad. It's just not a match. So you set it down and look for the YES, the match, the piece that fits exactly what you need in that moment. The certainty you have that there is a matching piece there somewhere is what frees you to treat it as simply not a match. You don't need to spend any additional time defending why you gave that piece a try. How it looked like a match and you were sure it was the right one, or trying to convince yourself it is good enough. Instead, you notice what about that piece made it not a match, add this to your knowledge about the puzzle, and you keep looking.

When you experience something and it is clear you don't want that thing, instead of being all frustrated and angry and thinking you just wasted your time, be grateful. Say, "Thank you, thank you, thank you!" The sooner you find out what you don't want, the faster you get to what you do want.

The path to our destination is not always a straight one.
We go down the wrong road, we get lost, we turn back.
Maybe it doesn't matter which road we embark on.
Maybe what matters is that we embark.

- Barbara Hall[23]

It's not required for you to go down the road of what you don't want to get to what you do want, just know if you do, there is always a gift of clarity and refinement available there for you.

What Are Maybes?

The talk with my friend Kurt that started this whole journey of following my YES got me wondering: If things are either YES or NO, then what are Maybes?

The more I explored this I realized Maybes are NOs we want to be YESES, but we are afraid they will not come back around, so we think we have to hold on to them and try and convert them into a YES right now.

Envision a merry-go-round. You spot the horse you want to ride but you missed your chance to jump on it when it came by. You could wait for it to come around again with confidence that if it is meant to be the horse you ride, it will be available when it comes back around and you'll get on it with ease. The first time it went by it wasn't quite a YES yet or you would already be on it.

The other approach is a Maybe.

You spot the horse you want to ride but something makes you hesitate. Instead of trusting that when it is your YES there will be no hesitation, you go chasing this Maybe. Worried there may never be anything this good again. Fearful that if you don't chase it down it will never come back around as a YES.

So, you put in all this effort and energy to chasing this Maybe down. You worry if you don't chase it now it won't be there when you need it.

Maybes happen when we don't
trust the Universe is on our side.

Maybes are when we try to force the Universe to give us what we want on our timeline, based on what our logical minds are telling us. What if we trusted that the Universe knows exactly what we need in this moment? Is that possible? Could it be the Universe is our biggest supporter and wants us to have everything we need to bloom and be completely fulfilled?

Sure, you spotted a horse you thought was the one for you, but perhaps it was just a representation of what's possible. If you keep your focus on only that which is a YES right now, it will lead you to a horse that is just as good or even better. But as long as you are chasing Maybes, your attention and your energy will be focused on the Maybe and you will miss your YES even when it is standing right in front of you.

Whenever you ask the Universe for anything it has one of three answers for you:

1. YES you can have that.
2. Not yet. (This is a Maybe.)
3. NO, because I have something better for you.

Psychotherapist and author Heide Banks[24] shared how she almost went chasing a Maybe and is so happy she didn't. When Heide met her husband they were living on different coasts. She lived in L.A. and he was in New York City. He wasn't quite out of his relationship, and he kept inviting her to come to New York where he lived. Going to visit him felt like a NO for her at that time. She could have made it a Maybe and gone chasing after it, but she didn't. There was a lot that this man had to disengage from. Heide's instincts told her to let him clean up his life before she entered it, so she followed this YES.

It took 6 months for him to get completely out of this relationship he had been in for 8 years. Heidi had made a vow to herself and followed her YES not to fly to New York to see him that entire time, and it wasn't easy.

As a result of following this guidance, when they got together it was very clean and there was nothing pulling on either of them.

Maybes are very insidious because they cut you off from your YESES. They are scarcity in action. If something or someone is not your YES in this moment, they will come back when they actually are your YES, just like what happened with Heidi and her husband. If they don't come back as a clear YES they aren't a match that supports you in blooming, someone or something else is.

Have you ever been to one of those sushi restaurants where they have a conveyor belt which brings the food around? It never fails that we take more food than we need or want.

We tell ourselves the Rainbow Roll may not come back around so we better grab it now even though we are just starting the appetizer course. And what happens, we end up grabbing way more food than we need because it looks good going by and perhaps we will want it in the future and we're afraid it will be gone by then, so we grab it now.

Following your YES is only taking the food you are ready to eat right now and trusting what you will need next will come around when you are ready for it. If the Rainbow Roll doesn't come back around, then it wasn't meant for you. Perhaps some unagi comes around instead, even better. (I love unagi, so this would definitely be an 'even better' moment for me.) The thing you can count on is the Universe will always have something just as good or even better on the conveyor belt of life when the time is right.

You can always tell if something is a Maybe by how much effort it takes. Maybes take tons of effort because you are trying to make what it is into something it isn't. You are trying to force a square peg into a round hole. It doesn't matter if you call it a "Maybe," a "sort of," a "kind of," a "could be," a "possibly," or a "not yet," it is still a NO you are trying to make into a YES.

— 9 —

Where do Maybes Come From?

How much time and energy do you spend trying to turn NOs into YESES? This is important to consider because trying to turn NOs into YESES is how we create Maybes.

We've all done this at one time or another. It's useful to be aware of how much we do this so we can recognize how much time and energy we are squandering on creating Maybes that would be more beneficially utilized building up your muscle of following your YES. One way to accelerate the development of your YES muscles is to recognize that just because something is not a YES right now, does not mean it never will be. Trying and force it into being a YES before its time leads to unnecessary pain, disappointment, and suffering. Here's what I mean:

The two appetizers my good friend Jill and I both love are calamari and hot, gooey cheese sticks. Due to COVID we had not been out to a restaurant in months and we were dying for these things so we decided to have some delivered. We both questioned this idea. We literally said out loud, "They probably won't be that good." But nonetheless, we called up our favorite restaurant and ordered them anyway.

To our surprise the delivery guy showed up faster than expected so we hoped our treats would still be hot. We tore open the to-go box, ripped the lid off the special dipping sauces and dove in.

Waa-waa! (Sad trombone).

Barely warm and dense, not gooey cheese filled our mouths. Hopefully the calamari would satisfy us. We both popped some in our mouths. Rubbery and cold, not delectable. As much as we desired these tasty treats, our YES was that getting them delivered would not satisfy this desire, and indeed it did not. We knew before we ever ordered them that having these favorite foods delivered was not our YES, but we did it anyway. We tried to make a NO into a YES. We were impatient for something we both clearly recognized as being a NO to be a YES now, and we paid the price. Do yourself a favor and follow your YESES. They will save you from the struggle and disappointment you experience when you chase Maybes.

WARNING! There is a place called Maybe-land and for many of us it feels familiar so our brain interprets it as safe, but it is the worst place you can possibly live.

— 10 —

Maybe-land

Maybe-land is the place where we cling to false hope instead of loving ourselves enough to follow our YES. This is where the voice in your head tries to convince you to settle by saying things like:

"Maybe these expectations are unrealistic."
"Maybe it's not so bad."
"Maybe it will change if I give it more time."
"Maybe I'm being too needy."
"Maybe this is better than nothing."

This is where you find yourself making up excuses, justifying disappointments, and pretending you don't want more — this is YOU abandoning YOU!

If Maybe-land is so bad, then why do we stay here?

We stay because we're scared.

We think if we just stay here long enough it will allay our fears that we are missing out on the life we are meant to live. We are afraid if we do something different we might fail or it won't turn out perfectly. We tell ourselves that something is better than nothing.

With this in mind let's revisit those Maybes -

"Maybe my expectations are unrealistic." - **What if they aren't?**

"Maybe it's not so bad." - **How bad does it need to get?**

"Maybe it will change if I give it more time." - **How much more time do you have?**

"Maybe I'm being too needy." - **Is a rose needy because it requires water to bloom? No, and your needs don't make you needy either.**

"Maybe this is better than nothing." - **"Nothing" doesn't suck the life out of you.**

When you're in Maybe-land your needs aren't being met. What you are doing doesn't completely align with you. It doesn't serve you. You're trying to force a NO into being a YES. This is not a judgment. It's simply facing the facts that where you are doesn't work for you right now. It may have served you in the past, but that doesn't mean you have to stay there if it no longer supports you in blooming and succeeding.

Maybe-land is the equivalent of eating a diet of nothing but coconuts and continually telling yourself. "Maybe this will work. Maybe this will satisfy all my dietary needs eventually. Maybe this will suddenly one day, pop into alignment, and my body will be thrilled that all I'm eating is coconuts."

Maybe-land is basically us denying what we know to be true for ourselves. Oftentimes we think a Maybe-land job, relationship, or friendship is better than nothing. The truth is, "nothing" doesn't suck the life out of you, but whatever you're in Maybe-land about, does. That thing you think is better than nothing is what's draining you. It could be your job, lifestyle, partner or anything.

The whole reason for following your YES is to bring the most complete expression of you to the world, to be the best you can be in this moment. If you're in Maybe-land, you're denying the truth that where you are is not supporting you in being your best. There's nothing to be ashamed of, that is unless you do nothing about it now that you know your in Maybe-land.

You cannot deny your way around your truth. Your truth is your essence. It is who you are at your core. We all have different truths, distinct individual needs, desires, passions and outcomes, we're here to support and manifest.

Your YESES are the directions you need to get out of Maybe-land and stay out forever.

— 11 —

A Life Without Maybes

Maybes are confidence killers. It's easy to get trapped worrying what people will think about us if we follow our YESES and NOS. Will we disappoint them? Will it hurt their feelings? Our concerns about how others will respond leads to unnecessary stress, hesitation and indecision.

The truth is we have no control over another's response. I have never known a YES or a NO that didn't ruffle a few feathers. Some people will like the choice you make and other's will not. That is just a fact of life.

If you want to be more certain, more confident and more decisive in your choices and actions you must eliminate Maybes from your life.

Think about what your life would be like without Maybes. No more overthinking. No more delaying your actions. No more denying what's true for you.

What if you could no longer deem anything a Maybe? From now on you only have a YES or NO option to identify things. Wouldn't your life be simpler?

How about we take a few minutes right now to eliminate Maybes from your life and find out?

Take a sheet of paper and divide it into three columns. At the top of the left-hand column write Maybes. At the top of the center column write NO and at the top of the right-hand column write the word YES like this:

Maybes	NO	YES

Take 2–3 minutes right now and write down whatever your current Maybes are.

Write down all the things you currently have in your Maybe category. Here are some possibilities to get you started:

- Maybe you will attend the party you were invited to.
- Maybe you should move.
- Maybe it is time to change careers.
- Maybe you should trade in your car and get a new one.
- Maybe the man or woman you've been dating isn't the one for you.

Since we just agreed to eliminate Maybes you must now put the items you have listed as Maybes in a different category. Use your pen to cross out the word Maybe, then take a few minutes right now and decide if what you have listed in the Maybe column are now a YES in this moment or a NO. Which one is it now that Maybe is no longer an option?

Rewrite each item in either the NO or YES column as you move it over cross out the item from the Maybe list.

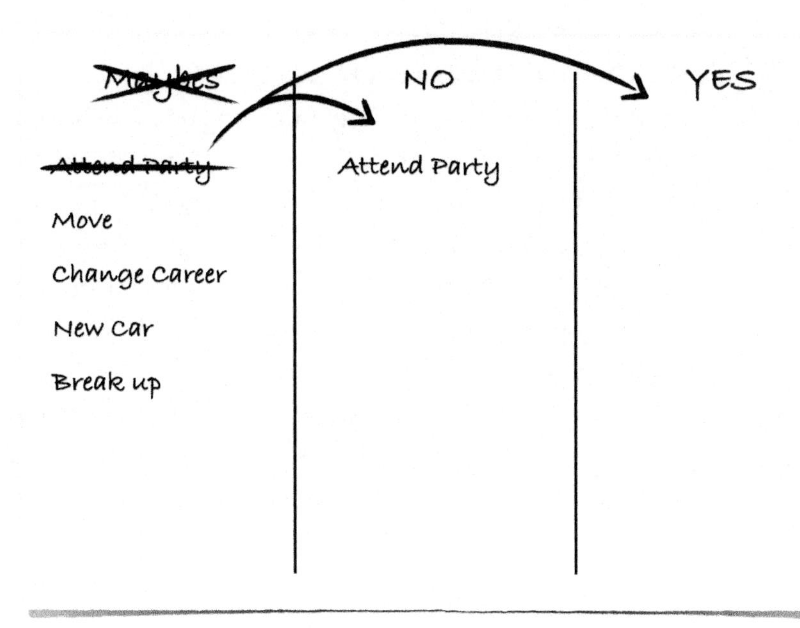

Great job! Look at that, you just eliminated Maybes from your life. Simple right?

What did you find? Did the things you had listed as Maybes move to being NOs or YESES?

Chances are they became NOs, because if they were truly YESES they would never have been in the Maybe category in the first place.

When I first started studying spirituality there was a teacher named Michael J. Tamura[25] who would come from California a couple times a year and lead workshops on various spiritual topics. Michael was my teacher's teacher, and it was very exciting when he came to town. Some of the students would go into a tizzy wondering if they should attend his workshops or not.

For me it was crystal clear. If it was my YES I would know right away and register for the class. If it was a NO for me, I would know right away and not give it another thought. I would be at peace and the decision was always easy to make because Maybe was not an option. For the students who still allowed Maybes in their lives they found themselves in the Hell of Maybe-land.

All they needed to do to escape this Hell was to choose if attending this event was a YES or a NO for them and not let Maybe be an option.

When you eliminate the option of letting something be a Maybe your life instantly becomes simpler. It holds you accountable. There is no middle ground for you to park things, or to avoid deciding if it is a NO or a YES. Choosing if something is a YES or a NO is really telling yourself the truth about what is in front of you. Getting out of your head and instead of trying to calculate if it's logical or the best strategic decision, you tune into what you're feeling in your heart about this.

By eliminating Maybes from your life you're not dismissing the fact that something has potential or it's a possibility or it could be a great option in the right circumstances. What you're recognizing is it's simply not a YES *right now*, and that's okay. This doesn't make it bad. It doesn't make you bad. It doesn't mean you gave up on it. It means you're following your YESES with the full knowledge that this thing, if it's meant to be your YES, will come back around in the right time and place.

So, you don't have to worry about it.

You don't have to force it.

You don't have to try and manipulate it and massage it and tolerate the current situation in hopes that somehow it will change and align with your truth.

If we're tolerating a current situation, or interaction, we're essentially telling others that this in fact *is* our YES, even when it's not. If you're going to put up with something unsupportive of you being your best then you are communicating, either by your words and/or your actions, that it works for you. It's like faking an orgasm. If you fake an orgasm, you're giving your partner the message that whatever they did provided the stimulation you needed for the pleasure, connection and release you desired.

If you just communicated to them that whatever they did works for you, then why would they try something else in the future? If their goal was to bring you pleasure they've just succeeded, and they are sure to repeat what they just did because, as far as they know, it worked.

When you're hanging out in Maybe-land you misrepresent what works for you. You communicate to the person or organization that what is currently going on is your YES when it's really your NO.

Do yourself a favor and be honest when you're making something a Maybe. Simply admit to yourself it is currently a NO which perhaps someday will be a YES, but it's not a YES right now. No harm, no foul. By removing the option of something being a Maybe it clarifies the YESES that support you in blooming in this moment. It also eliminates the anxious, nervous, undecided version of you that exists as long as you allow Maybes to exist and keep hanging out in Maybe-land. Now isn't that worth removing one word from your vocabulary?

The Follow Your YES Formula

Now that we've clarified what Maybes, NOs and YESES are, it's time to put this all together and take your first pass at following your YES. I've included simple action steps to show you the way. Following your YES is a process, it's not a do it once and you're done kind of thing. It's not a wait for a giant epiphany kind of thing either. It's a day-to-day practice of tuning in to your YES in the moment.

Know that you'll have days it seems second nature, and you'll have days where it seems like the last thing you want or can do. Therefore, we continue to practice. I've been doing this for more than twenty years and there are still days where I'll recognize I haven't been following my YES. Perhaps I got caught up in the momentum of the situation and forgot to check in with myself. This happens. Life happens. No matter how committed you are to something, we all regress at times and this is when we have to recommit.

Be aware as you start you could feel like you don't have a YES. You might feel like you can't find your YES. The truth is we all have a YES *for this moment*. Typically, when I work with people, and they say, "I don't have anything," or "I don't see anything," or "I don't get anything," what they're really saying is what they're getting for a YES is not what they expected. When this happens we tend to dismiss what we do get because we thought we knew what our YES was going to be right then, and when it doesn't show up like we expected, we say there's nothing there.

For instance, if I had you close your eyes, and then asked you what you see, you might say "I don't see anything." And then if I said, "Then tell me what you DO see?" You might say "All I see is black." Well, then black is what you're seeing, isn't it? It's just not what you expected to see. You might have thought you'd see colors or an image of some type or something profound. Just know that whatever is showing up for you is correct. Trust that there's a reason beyond your current understanding for the YES you're receiving and be amused. Amusement dissolves all the seriousness of "I don't get anything" or "I'm not doing this right" so things flow more easily. Find your amusement, a grin, a "Sheesh!," a laugh or a snort whenever you're feeling a struggle, and check to see if you're smiling. If not, let yourself smile, and relax into your amusement.

When you first learned to drive you had to consciously think about how to drive. You probably took a driver's education course to learn how to properly turn a corner, how to depress the accelerator so you took off without a jolt and how hard to press on the brake to stop smoothly, etc. Back then you had to actively think about steering, accelerating and braking, but now it's second nature. This is exactly how you are going to master following your YES.

The formula may look daunting right now, much like driving a car may have felt when you first got behind the wheel. Know that with consistent practice, following your YES will become natural and second nature, but it will take practice. So as you read this formula, know that soon what now takes reading the instructions to perform will become something you do by thinking of a simple phrases or even a single acronym like FYY. Sit back, enjoy learning and know that soon this will be as automatic as driving a car.

Be a beginner. When you're a beginner,
any step you take is a success.

- Emily Pereira

— 12 —

Permission to Be a Beginner

If you want to enjoy developing your ability to follow your YES you must give yourself permission to be a beginner.

Because we have a certain number of years of experience being a human, it's tempting to feel like we should already be at our goal. We want to jump ahead, even when doing something new. We can't imagine being a beginner at this stage in life. Being a beginner can be clumsy, awkward and embarrassing. The idea of being all those things again, as we were when we were growing up, is uncomfortable. We want to be at the finish line now, and there are two ways to reach the finish line.

We can begin at the start line and take the required steps along the course, enjoying the journey as we go that ultimately culminates in the feelings of joy and accomplishment as we cross the finish line. Or we can go sit by the finish line and watch others who ran the race finish.

The difference is either being a participant or a spectator in life. Which do you prefer?

In 2006 I participated in something called Steps Across America and walked from New York to California to commemorate 50 years of the Presidential Counsel on Fitness and inspire kids to be more active. It was one of my long-term YESES. For some reason, ever since I was a little kid, I had wanted to cross the country like this. Plus, being able to share the message of health and fitness while fulfilling this YES was a bonus.

As a healthy and active 39-year-old who had been walking most my life I thought the walking would be no big deal. One day I decided a little training might be a good idea so I walked to my girlfriend's house about 2 miles away. I woke up the next morning and I could barely move.

I had committed to walking 20 to 25 miles day after day and a 2-mile stroll across town had just kicked my ass. I wondered if I had bitten off more than I could chew. There was only one way I was going to be able to fulfill this YES. I had to be a beginner and start by doing short walks of just a couple of miles, which then developed into longer walks of 5 miles, then 10 miles, until I could walk 20 miles without much difficulty.

When we arrived at Chelsea Pier in New York City I had to be a beginner all over again. Walking along highways and through cities as we navigated a route we had never seen before while watching out for all kinds of hazards like vehicles turning, holes in the sidewalk, protective dogs running out of yards to chase us, and countless other distractions was very different from walking on quiet paths and trails in the desert outside of Sedona, Arizona, where I lived at the time.

Over and over, I let myself be a beginner. Walking in busy cities, in rural areas, over mountains, across deserts and countless other beginner opportunities kept presenting themselves. I promise you that when 2,800 miles later we arrived at Santa Monica Pier having taken over 6,700,000 steps (we actually counted) I was so glad I had given myself permission to be a beginner again and again. There were friends and family who had been at Chelsea Pier when we started who were now at Santa Monica Pier to welcome us as we finished, and I guarantee you their experience as spectators was nothing like our experience as participants. On this walk I got blisters, sore muscles, made wrong turns, ended up on an interstate by accident and had to be escorted off by the police. It was anything but perfect, and the key to completing this walk was letting myself be a beginner.

Part of being a beginner is granting yourself permission to witness others as being ahead of you without thinking where they are in their journey means you are behind in yours.

Towards the end of my walk across America I started thinking about running a marathon. Please understand, I was not a runner. In fact, when people used to ask me if I wanted to go for a run I would reply that I only ran when being chased. Running was not an interest, passion or desire of mine. However, one of my fellow walkers Richard, trained people to go from being a couch potato to running a marathon, and he assured me I would be able to complete a marathon with relative ease, as long as I trained for it. He recommended a book called *The Non-Runner's Marathon Trainer* which sounded perfect for me since I was an adamant non-runner. I knew I would never have more miles in my legs than I did after walking across the country, so if I was ever going to run a marathon this was the time.

After we completed our walk in Santa Monica, I took a little time off to let my body recover and then signed up for the California International Marathon in Sacramento, California, bought the book Richard had recommended, and started training. I want to be clear about how much I was **not** a runner prior to this point. In Boulder, Colorado, where I live now, there is something called the BOLDERBoulder. It's a 10K race held on Memorial Day and over 50,000 people of all shapes and sizes show up from all over the country to participate. Olympic medal winners, grandparents, running enthusiasts, average Jills and Joes and kids of all ages come together to run a course lined with bands, belly dancers, an Elvis impersonator as well as people handing out free beers, bacon and even cotton candy. Yet with all the fun surrounding this event, I had never run it. Not even free beer and bacon could get me to run, and I love both those things.

So there I was having just walked hundreds and hundreds of miles from one coast to the other and guess where I started out with my marathon training ... at the beginning. I soon found out, walking and running employ muscles in different ways. Though I could now easily walk twenty-five miles in a just a few hours, running a couple of miles was brutal. Fast forward to marathon race day after being a beginner at running 2 miles and then a beginner at running 3 miles, then 5 miles all the way up to my longest training run of 20 miles. Now it was time to be a beginner at running 26.2 miles.

The race was a mass start, meaning everyone started at the same time. It was pretty exciting to be there with 2,000 other people of all abilities on that cold December morning and think we were all about to run this course together. The fastest runners and the slowest runners were all within a few feet of each other as the starter's gun went off. I soon found my pace and was feeling pretty good about my progress until we reached the midway point at 13.1 miles. As we approached this point in the race one of the other runners said, "the winners just finished." My brain scrambled for a minute thinking, how could this be? We'd all started together a short while ago. But it was true, some of the people I started with ran twice as fast as I did. I started to smile and then laugh.

By letting myself be a beginner over and over again it freed me from the pain of comparison. I could recognize someone being faster or further along than I was at the very same task and enjoy both their success and my progress.

Giving yourself permission to be a beginner sets you free to run your own race. Start small, take baby steps as you practice following your YES. Working on tasks that are on the edge of your current abilities will help you stay motivated. Expecting to go from couch potato to marathon runner overnight will demoralize you. I trained for five months for my marathon, and that was after spending 3.5 months walking across the country and I was thrilled with my time of 4 hours and 20 minutes even though the winners finished in half the time I did. Celebrate being a beginner, build momentum, strengthen your YES following muscles, and enjoy the journey.

Start by doing something as simple as trusting your internal guidance, your YES, to guide you in what to wear tomorrow, what to order the next time you go out to eat or get coffee, or which route to drive to work in the morning. Then notice how you feel following your YES. Are you confident, nervous, relaxed, hesitant, excited? Just notice what it feels like when you follow your YES as a beginner and let this be enough for now.

It's the rare person who can go from laying on the couch doing nothing to running a marathon and winning it. They are the ones who fascinate us, so we hear about them the most. You are extraordinary in your own way. Do not discount what your life looks like because it doesn't look like the people you see on TV or in magazines or on social media. Allow yourself to find your pace.

The thing that is really hard, and really amazing, is giving up on being perfect and beginning the work of becoming yourself.

- Anna Quindlen[26]

When you give yourself permission to be a beginner no matter how long you have been doing something you will always feel successful. There's always going to be a next level where you are a beginner. This is true of all growth. Honor being a beginner in your career, your relationships, your health or anything else and you will free yourself to grow without judgement.

— 13 —

No Such Thing as an Insignificant YES

Another thing to be aware of as you start following your YES is that there are primarily two kinds of YESES. The big-holy-cow-life-changing YESES — where you have a great big epiphany for a new direction with your health, career, lifestyle or relationship etc. There are also the everyday kind of YESES. These are much more common. They literally happen multiple times every day. Guiding you on what to eat, where to go, who to talk to, what to do next and so on.

Oftentimes we feel like the only ones that matter are the big-holy-cow version. However it is the everyday variety that make up the vast majority of our lives. The more we pay attention to the everyday YESES and follow them, the quicker we build our YES following muscles and the easier it is to recognize and follow the holy-cow YESES when they arrive. Even when the guidance you receive is quieter or seems less significant, know they are all of equal importance to living a life full of ease and fulfillment.

CEO and Co-Founder of 9Q Solutions, Dr. Laura Ciel[27], shares how treating some YESES as insignificant can sabotage us from being able to show up as our best self in all circumstances -

> *"When there are a lot of things going on, it gets busy and I'm just taking everything on, and not pausing to check and see what do I need to do to make sure I'm set up to handle this in the best way possible I*

pay the price. It can be an accumulation of small moments where I'm not listening to my intuition, I'm not listening to my YES. The size of the guidance doesn't matter.

For me I need to be out in nature, I need to have physical activity, it's one of those things that really helps me when things are tough. It helps me with my kids, it helps me in my relationships, and my work. You personally might have different things which are important to you - a bath, dancing, music, a walk, or whatever it is for you.

If I don't pay attention when my YES is telling me,"Hey, you need a little time alone, and you need a little time out hiking on the trail, or you need to go for a swim." If I neglect that once possibly I don't feel that great. If I continue to not pay attention, I will get really cranky, and I will not be able to do what I need to do in any of my relationships.

Start to train yourself to listen to your YES as soon as possible. If something just doesn't feel quite right, stop before you take action.

When I stop and I check in and follow my guidance, I come back exactly where I need to be for whatever is in front of me at that particular time, whether it is personal or work.

What people tend to do, and what I used to do, is tell myself that's not practical. I don't have enough time. Somehow it's not acceptable to follow my YES right now.

Listen to your YES, because nurturing yourself is part of taking responsibility for who you are and how you show up in the world."

As humans we tend to want big shifts. What we fail to remember is the big shifts often happen as the result of many little incremental movements, little changes. These little changes look tiny in the big scheme of things, but what they lead to, is enormous.

A journey of a thousand miles begins with a single step

- Lao-tzu[28]

Think of each of your YES as a single domino in a long line of dominos that make up a very intricate pattern. You've probably seen videos of these kind of domino designs online. What happens if you remove one of the dominos from the pattern? We learned this playing as children. It interrupts the flow, and if you remove enough of them you destroy the interconnectedness which makes the flow of the design work.

The Universe has its eye on the big picture for you. It has a much more expansive view than any of us can see. So even when a YES seems insignificant to you, trust that it plays an integral role in keeping the flow going in your life.

I encourage you to take a couple minutes and watch a video of dominos falling. There is a great one on YouTube called The Amazing Triple Spiral[29] that provides an excellent visual of how one YES leads to the next and ultimately creates something extraordinary. (Take a couple minutes to watch it now.)

Notice how in The Amazing Triple Spiral video the majority of the dominos are standard sized dominos, but there are a handful of bigger ones at about the 1:23 mark in the video. Observe how even though those few dominos are much larger in size, their role is still the same. By each domino tipping forward just a little bit, it contributes to the continuation of this series of events that is dramatic, beautiful, and definitely significant. The same is true for each one of your YESES. We get to our ultimate goals by embracing that those little incremental changes have value. The guidance you receive may be as seemingly pointless as tipping forward just a little bit like the domino did. Not some great big action like starting a business or moving across the country, but simply tipping over and moving forward just a smidge. This action connects you to your next YES and then the one after that until all of a sudden, everything picks up momentum. It takes all these little YESES, one after another, to ultimately lead to the final goal of living a life filled with ease, excitement and accomplishment.

Don't dismiss the incremental steps. By simply following your YESES no matter how life-changing or trivial they may seem, you tap into the natural flow that is already laid out for you. The Divine has already set up your dominos for you in a series of YESES that make up a happy and satisfying life. Your job is to honor each one as equally important and acknowledge there is no such thing as an insignificant YES.

STEP ONE

Look with Different Eyes

In order to successfully follow your YES you must look with different eyes. We typically are motivated to do things because we expect to feel better as the result of taking an action. To follow your YES you must look for that feeling. I realize this may sound like a strange idea, so let me show you what I mean.

This past summer, I took a trip back to the Midwest to visit my family. I had a very early flight and as I pulled out of my driveway in the 4 a.m. darkness, I got a YES that came through as, "Feel upgraded." "Feel upgraded," I had no idea what this meant, but I liked the way it felt. I thought, "Yeah, I want to feel upgraded on this trip." Something told me this was more than simply getting the seat on my flight upgraded, so I decided to keep my radar tuned to "feeling upgraded." I decided to look for this feeling everywhere I went.

It's normally about a 45-minute drive to the airport through metropolitan Denver and on this drive, I only hit one red light. It was the smoothest, nearly nonstop drive to the airport I remember.

I was like, *Wow, that felt upgraded.*

Then I arrived at the parking facility where I had a reservation. It was now about 4:30 in the morning and as I pulled up, a young man came out of the office and ran up to the gate where I was supposed to enter my access code. I thought there might be something wrong with the machine, so I rolled down my window and he said, "Do you have a reservation with us sir?" I confirmed I did. Then he said, "I apologize but we overbooked our outside parking so we've upgraded you to indoor valet parking at no additional cost. Please pull into row H, and there'll be a shuttle there to pick you up." He literally said "upgraded." He used that exact word. I was only 45 minutes into a weeklong trip, and I'd already felt upgraded twice.

This was fun.

I won't go into all the details, but there were at least six more things that happened on the way to visit my family where I felt upgraded. I was very pleased with myself for paying attention to my YES and following it.

As I was getting ready to return to Colorado a week later, I wondered if I could have an upgraded experience going home. I wondered if feeling upgraded was still available. I couldn't imagine why not, and I decided to do the same thing as I did on the first leg of my trip and be tuned into feeling upgraded and looking for that feeling. I took the train up to Chicago where I was going to catch my flight. It was a very busy platform which was kind of surprising. It looked to me like this would be a full train. As I approached the train the conductor was helping people on and directing passengers to this side or that side based on their final destination. He looks at me and said, "If you go to the second car to the left you'll find a lot more seats available." Sounded good to me, so I walked through the first car which was jammed with groups of school kids and families. To my surprise there were only four people in the second car and only two more arrived later. It was peaceful, relaxing and I had plenty of room to stretch out. I felt upgraded.

I thought the real test to feeling upgraded would be at Midway airport. I was flying Southwest, an airline I really enjoy flying. However, on Southwest they only have one class of seating, there is no first class or business class, so I knew I wouldn't be getting my seating class upgraded. Nor do they do assigned seating. I received my boarding position, which determined the order people can get on the plane, and I got the worst position I'd ever been given ... C-43. This meant 162 people would board before I did, and there were only 180 seats on the plane. How was I going to possibly feel upgraded on this flight, I wondered.

For those of you who've never met me, I'm not a small man. I'm six-foot three inches tall, with broad shoulders and I weigh around 200 pounds. Sitting in the middle seat is not ideal for me, nor is it for anybody sitting next to me. I was sure this was going to be a middle seat flight and I was dreading it. I intentionally decided to stay tuned into feeling upgraded. I didn't know how it was going to turn out. But I didn't know I was going to get upgraded at the parking area or have all those green lights or the conductor would help me find a peaceful seat on the train either, and they turned out great. I watched everybody else board the plane and they finally called "Group C seats 31–60" and I started making my way on board.

When I stepped on the plane I looked all the way to the back of the plane hoping to find a window or aisle seat open. The flight attendant at the door said something to me and I turned around to answer, and that's when I noticed the very first seat in the front row was empty. The seat belt was laid across the seat untouched and I thought "how could this row one seat still be available?"

I looked at the women who were sitting in the other two seats and said, "Is this seat open?" The woman in the middle seat replied "Yes, you can sit there." And I literally said out loud, with a big smile on my face, "Yes, I can!" and sat down in my front row aisle seat.

Now if I'm honest, my mind was racing with thoughts of this is too good to be true. This seat couldn't still be available. Why would all those people have passed up such a great seat? I expected to be told it was being held for somebody or the person sitting there was in the bathroom. My logical brain was convinced this couldn't last. Then I caught myself and realized this kind of thinking was not helpful. I refocused on what I *did* want, and kept saying to myself "This is my seat. This is my seat. This is my seat." A few minutes later they closed the door to the plane, and this front row aisle seat was indeed my seat. My "feeling upgraded" festival continued!

I had one of the last boarding positions to get on the plane and somehow ended up at the very first seat. I was going to be the first person off the plane and I got an aisle seat with tons of legroom. Even on an airline where there isn't technically an upgrade, I still felt upgraded.

Do you see how I was looking with different eyes on this trip?

I could have looked at all the ways things were going to be difficult. Travel was more difficult with COVID than it used to be and not having some of the things I used to enjoy about going to the airport could have made this trip a struggle that I would just have to endure.

Instead, I followed my YES and looked to "feel upgraded." Even though I didn't know what "feel upgraded" really meant, I trusted it would be there and I would recognize it when I saw it. I kept doing this through every segment of my trip. Which resulted in me sitting in, what I would consider, one of the best seats on the entire plane even though I was one of the last people to board.

Looking with different eyes is a key component which allows you to actually be able to follow your YES. You've got to be looking for it. You've got to be trusting it's out there and it's available to you. Trust you're worthy of receiving it, and you can have it at any time if you're paying attention and your attention is on the feeling of what you **do** want, instead of what you don't want.

Make your future dream a present fact by assuming the feeling of the wish fulfilled.

- Wayne Dyer[30]

ACTION STEP ONE

Since we live in a physical world we are used to looking for things, casting our gaze for forms, not for feelings. For this step you are going to be resetting your radar to look for feelings instead of forms. The way you shift this is when you catch yourself focusing on tangible outcomes, like landing a new client or losing ten pounds or receiving flowers from an admirer, stop and check in with your heart. Ask yourself how are you expecting to feel as a result of receiving or experiencing the form you're focused on? You might imagine that when you land a new client you will feel successful, when you lose ten pounds you'll feel healthy or sexy, when you receive flowers you will feel loved and cared about. Now reset your radar to look for feeling successful, healthy, loved or whatever the feeling is for you, just as I did when I looked to "feel upgraded" on my trip.

By focusing on the feeling, you become open to experiencing it regardless of the form it takes. The Universe loves to surprise us with something better than we could have imagined, but we must be looking for the feeling or we will walk right by the form when it presents itself.

As one of the last 20 people to board my flight I honestly had started to lose my focus on feeling upgraded and was focusing instead on finding a form — a seat — that wouldn't be too miserable to sit in for the two-and-a-half hour flight. So I almost walked right past the best seat on the plane. I was already looking to the back of the plane searching for the form I expected my seat to take. I almost missed out on the "something better" part the Universe had available for me. Feelings take many forms if we will let them.

— 14 —

Where is Your YES Leading You?

Many people get stymied by the desire to know what will happen if they follow their YES. They want to know where their YES is taking them before they will follow it. This will stop you from blooming every time. No one can tell you what will happen with absolute certainty because there are too many variables at play. If certainty is a pre-requisite for you, you are dead in the water before you even get started. (Oh, and even if they could tell you with certainty, you would never believe it.)

Henry Ford had an 8th grade education and yet he changed the world. He didn't do what he did because he wanted to change the world though, he simply had a natural mechanical aptitude and could not contain his interest in building and improving things. By following his YES and sharing his gifts he developed the assembly line technique of mass production that transformed the automobile from a plaything for the wealthy to a tool for everyone, and in so doing he had a massive and lasting impact on nearly every person on the planet.

Imagine if, before Henry followed his YES to implement the assembly line in the manufacture of his cars, the Divine told him that when he followed this YES he would be able to manufacture 25 cars a day instead of it taking a day-and-a-half to manufacture just one. And that eventually his company would grow to the point where a new car would be coming off the line of one of his factories every 10 seconds. Do you think he would have believed it? No, that would have been so far beyond comprehension in Henry's day that he would have thought it was crazy talk. And yet this is exactly what happened.

When Oprah Winfrey was growing up in Mississippi she had no idea she was going to be "Oprah Winfrey." I doubt she was sitting there thinking, "Unless I know that by following my YES I will become a billionaire and impact the world on a global scale with virtually every word I say, I'm not doing it." Instead she trusted, followed her YES, and blossomed into her true self, only then were her gifts available to be received by millions of people. In both cases they followed their YES and bloomed into their true expressions so they could share the gifts of who they were and as a result had a huge impact on the world.

If we knew what was available to us when we followed our YES it would blow our minds. Simply trust that the Divine is guiding you towards your highest good and proceed. The simplest and indeed the only way to have your greatest impact on the world is to follow your YES. To be the fullest expression of you regardless of what anyone else is doing or saying or thinking and celebrate you. Never hold back on following your YES because you can't tell where it is leading you. Who knows, the YES you follow today just might be the key to you becoming the next Oprah or Henry Ford.

Most of the time we don't know where a YES is leading us. Henry and Oprah didn't know either. You may think you know, but it may surprise you and often does. Stay open to what the YES could bring, regardless of whether it appears to follow the path you thought you were on or not.

I don't know where I'm going from here, but I promise it won't be boring.

- David Bowie[31]

Can you follow your NOs or your Maybes without knowing where they're leading you? Of course you can. We've all done this countless times.

If we knew where they were leading us we would never follow them, would we? The point is you don't need to know where your YES is leading you before you follow it.

According to a recent Yale University study,[32] it's actually good not to know because uncertainty signals the brain to kickstart learning. The study basically concluded that if you're not at least a little stressed about the outcome of what you're doing, your brain shuts down learning. In many areas of life we want to continually improve and learn, and to do that you need to avoid the easy and comfortable in favor of the unpredictable.

The original *Karate Kid* movie "wax on wax off" scene is a great lesson in following your YES even when you don't know where it is taking you.

Mr. Miyagi, is the personification of the Divine, and Daniel, the teenage boy who keeps getting beat up at school, represents you and me. Daniel's YES is to learn karate from Mr. Miyagi, but he quickly feels deceived because he can't see how what Mr. Miyagi is teaching him has anything to do with learning karate. If you are familiar with this movie, you may remember when Mr. Miyagi agrees to teach Daniel karate he says:

> **Mr. Miyagi:** *First make sacred pact. I promise teach karate. That my part. You promise learn. I say, you do, no questions. That your part. Deal?*
>
> **Daniel:** *It's a deal.*
>
> **Mr. Miyagi:** *First wash all the cars, then wax.*
>
> **Daniel:** *Why do I have to...*
>
> **Mr. Miyagi:** *Remember deal. No questions.*
>
> **Daniel:** *Yeah, but--*
>
> **Mr. Miyagi:** *Wax on right hand. Wax off left hand. Wax on, wax off. Breathe in through nose, out through mouth. Wax on, wax off. Don't forget to breathe. Very important. Wax on, wax off. Wax on, wax off.*

Daniel proceeds to wash and wax all the cars. Then he paints the fence, paints the house, and sands the floors. After four days of this Daniel is fed up and starts yelling at Mr. Miyagi:

Daniel: *"We made a deal here. You're supposed to teach and I'm supposed to learn remember? For four days I've been busting my ass and haven't learned a goddamn thing.*

Mr. Miyagi: *Ah you learned plenty.*

Daniel: *I learned plenty? I learned how to sand your decks maybe. I learned how to wash your car, paint your house, paint your fence. I learned plenty, right.*

Mr. Miyagi: *Not everything is as seems.*

Daniel: *Oh bullshit! I'm going home.*

Mr. Miyagi calls Daniel back and proceeds to show him how what he learned from wax on wax off, paint the fence, paint the house, and sand the floor was actually conditioning Daniel for defensive karate without his foreknowledge of it. Mr. Miyagi saw the bigger picture. The key to this whole transformation was the sacred pact he made with Mr. Miyagi. It's the "I say, you do, no questions" part of this pact that is the most important. Your YES will not always make sense to you in the moment. Our job is to trust the Divine. Trust that God, the Universe, Great Spirit or whatever you call the higher power has your back and is guiding you on the best path for you to grow, expand and bloom. Believing your YES is showing you the shortcut to love, success and happiness even when you can't see it from where you're standing will change your life.

Now you may be thinking of course this works in the movies but what about for the rest of us who live in the real world? A completely valid concern, so let me give you a couple more examples. One from my life and another from a friend's.

A couple of years ago I was flying back from Boston, and as I was queuing up to board the plane they were asking if anyone was willing to give up their seat. Something told me this was a YES for me. Now, because trusting my YES is an ongoing practice I can struggle with it as well. My brain immediately kicked in to do its thing and evaluate if this action "made sense". It very quickly ran through various considerations:

- Did it matter if I got home late tonight or early tomorrow? - No.
- Was there anything on my calendar that would be negatively affected by this change? - No.
- Would I incur additional expenses as the result of giving up my seat? - No.

This all checked out with my rational mind, but I knew I needed a place to stay. I did not have a hotel, nor did I live in Boston. My YES was that I could help them take care of one of their other customers by giving up my seat, as long as I felt taken care of. If the airlines would provide a place for me to stay I was willing to give up my seat. So I walked up to the agent, and let her know, I'd be willing to give up my seat as long as they had a hotel room for me. She immediately escorted me over to the ticket counter, and let them know the situation and my specific needs in order to be able to give up my seat. The woman at the counter looked at me and said, "You got it. We have one hotel room left, and I'm going to give it to you. We just had to cancel a flight to Cleveland which means they are all going to have to stay over and there's no way we can put them all in one hotel room. So I'm giving you the room." The Universe was supporting me in following my YES.

As she's telling me this, the gentleman who was desperately trying to get on my flight to Denver overhears the conversation, walks up to me, and thanks me profusely. By giving up my seat, it was going to allow him to make it to a relative's wedding on time. He had missed flights all day long, because of weather issues, and my flight was the last opportunity for him to be there for the ceremony. I gotta say, following my YES felt pretty good right then.

The next day, when I returned to the airport, the TSA agent at security recognized and greeted me. I was carrying a box of cannolis from world famous Mike's Pastry, and the agent joked with me that they were contraband, and he would have to confiscate them. It was the friendliest exchange I have ever had at security.

Then as I'm walking through the terminal the gate agent I had spoken with the night before when I volunteered to give up my seat spotted me. She crossed the terminal to say hello, and escorted me to my gate, walking me to the front of the line and allowing me to board the plane early as a reward for giving up my seat the night before.

Over 50,000 people go through Logan Airport in Boston every day, yet because I followed one YES, I felt like I was special, and not just another faceless traveler. I was recognized and greeted in a way that was very different.

Oh, and the other immediate bonus following my YES led to was the night before when they made the adjustment on my ticket, they refunded half of my original ticket since I was not taking that part of my trip. Then they gave me a free flight home, and on top of that they awarded me $800 in credit towards future travel.

I hadn't even thought about receiving payment for giving up my seat, this was a total windfall. Now the reason I mentioned the travel credit is a few months later there was 100-year flood where I lived in Colorado and in that flood, I lost my home and my car.

The travel vouchers I had been awarded more than covered all the travel I needed to take to complete the rest of the personal development program I was taking. After the loss of my car and my home and all the unexpected expenses associated with that loss, I'm not sure I would have been able to complete my program if I hadn't had those vouchers to fall back on.

Unbeknownst to me, my YES of giving up my seat on that flight led me to:

- Assisting someone in attending a wedding.
- Feeling at home and welcomed in a major international airport, where 1000s of people are walking through and somehow I was being greeted as if I was family.
- Being escorted to the front line and first aboard the plane.

- Receiving vouchers which covered the entire travel for the rest of the year, so I could complete a program even though I experienced a major loss 3 months later due to the flood.

You never know what following your YES is going to open up for you. Give yourself the opportunity to find out. The Divine has so much in store for us than we can possibly understand. As you give yourself permission to receive each YES in the moment you open yourself to golden opportunities for more rewards yet to come.

My friend, Peter Schutte, is a world renowned photographer and his class is the reason I was in the rose garden in Portland to take pictures on the morning I discovered the rose analogy I've been sharing with you. Over a series of classes I took with him we got to know each other and through our friendship I learned he did not plan to be a photographer at all. Peter was from Holland and he came to the U.S. to study for a doctorate in math and physics at Northwestern University in Chicago. This was during the Cold War and one day while working in the lab with his fellow students it became clear to them the work they were doing was going to be used for military applications, and since he was a Quaker and a pacifist, he immediately went to the Dean of his department and withdrew from the program. It was clear that withdrawing from the Ph.D program was his YES. Unfortunately, this led to him falling into a period of depression as he did not know what to do with his life anymore. One day he saw a poster announcing Ansel Adams was going to give a lecture and show his photos. At the time, Ansel Adams was not well-known and Peter had never heard of him, but something told him he needed to attend the lecture. Here's what happened in Peter's own words:

> *It was a bitterly cold and windy evening in Chicago, and Adams gave a terrible lecture. He was reading verbatim from a manuscript, but he would look up and try to make eye contact with the audience. Then he would lose his place in the manuscript and ended up making excuses and jokes about it. This happened over and over again, and I walked out of that lecture three times that evening. But there was a blizzard going on outside, and it was so cold that I went back in again.*

By the time I returned the third time Ansel had finished his horrible lecture and was showing slides of his photography. I recognized one of the photos and something told me I needed to speak with him.

After the presentation I approached him and told him I needed to talk with him. To my surprise he invited me to meet him at his hotel the next day and gave me the address.

I thought we would spend a half hour or so talking, but that meeting took up the entire afternoon; and he took me to dinner, also. He encouraged me to pursue photography, as long as I was not acting on an impulse. Then he gave me a piece of advice that I have remembered to this day. He said a person has to do what they love; and that really hit me because I was giving up on math, which I had loved.

Adams recommended Peter study at the Rochester Institute of Technology Photo School, so he moved to Rochester, New York, and began taking classes.

A couple of years later, after completing his studies in Rochester, Peter was living in New York City and struggling to make it as a photographer. During his conversation with him in Chicago Ansel had given Peter his phone number and an open invitation to visit him at his home in Carmel, California. Peter called Ansel Adams. Here's how he describes the call:

I called Adams, but he said he no longer remembered who I was. Fortunately, Adams's wife was near the phone; and she remembered that her husband had mentioned me. She then made him hold his word and invited me to their home.

Peter bought a used VW, loaded everything he owned in it and drove from NYC to California. What started as a two-week stay continued for nearly a year where Peter was their guest and an assistant to Adams at his workshops in Yosemite. As you might imagine his time with Ansel Adams put Peter on an upward trajectory as a photographer including being awarded the position of official portrait photographer of the European Union in 1992. In this role he has photographed all the kings, queens, presidents and prime ministers of the EU. All of this started with Peter following his YES.

Peter reflected to me that virtually every time he has had a big YES and followed it, things start off rocky, but by staying true to his YES the end result is always far beyond anything he could have imagined. When you open your heart and follow your YES you'll be amazed where it will lead you.

FOLLOW YOUR YES FORMULA

STEP ONE
Look with Different Eyes

ACTION STEP - Tune into the feeling of your YES instead of the form you expect it to take, just as I looked to "feel upgraded" on my trip.

The Universe loves to surprise us with something better than we could have imagined, but we have to be looking for the feeling or we will walk right by the form when it presents itself.

Often times we don't know where a YES is leading us. Stay open to what the YES could bring, regardless of whether it appears to follow the path you thought you were on or not.

STEP TWO
Release Resistance

STEP THREE
Two Simple Questions

(You can download a printable version of the complete formula cheat sheet at followyouryes.com/cheatsheet)

Not believing is resistance to believing.

STEP TWO

Release Resistance

Following your YES requires a breakthrough. This is where you break through your own resistance to your reality. Don't take your reality and try and improve it through resistance to what it is. Instead step into your dream space where there is no resistance. When you dream you don't resist what you are dreaming. You don't think, "How can that be? I don't even know George Clooney, what would I be doing at his wedding? Wait, isn't he already married? And where did this gorgeous +1 I'm with come from?"

When you are dreaming you have no resistance to what is possible.

Give yourself permission to have the same freedom from resistance while you are awake, that you have in your dream space.

Resistance often stems from us thinking we need to know *how* something will happen before we are open to it happening. When I received the YES that morning as I pulled out of my driveway to feel upgraded on my trip I had a momentary response of "Now how's that going to happen?"

Then I shifted and I thought, "Why do I care *how* it happens. I'm excited to feel upgraded. I expect to feel upgraded. Now I know what to be looking for." You might say, hitting mostly green lights early in the morning is not uncommon, and you may be right. But if it's common or uncommon is not important. What matters is how did I feel as a result of the experience.

When you look with different eyes, as you learned about in STEP 1, you expect that which aligns with your truth, your YES, to be there.

We often resist believing the Universe is always providing limitless support to us.

It may be easy to believe the Universe is supporting you in small things, like finding your keys, having traffic move just fast enough to make it to work on time or the weather clearing up so it doesn't ruin your picnic. But for what we deem to be "big things" like finding a dream job or the perfect romantic partner, we can struggle and doubt the Universe is there for us in the same way. Our confidence in the support diminishes.

This lack of confidence is what I call Too Good To Be True Syndrome or TGTBT Syndrome for short.

You're wanting something but you don't believe you can actually have it. So when it shows up, you resist its validity. We've been taught to struggle and grind and that things of value take effort so when something shows up with ease we get suspicious. Here's how TGTBT Syndrome displayed itself for a woman I was working with named Terri, who had developed a very clear vision of what she was looking for in a romantic partner. She decided to see what would happen, now that we had been working together for a while, if she got back on an online dating site. Literally within the first hour of her profile being active she got contacted by a man whose profile had everything Terri was looking for. She said she was flabbergasted by how quickly he had appeared.

This is when her TGTBT Syndrome showed up. She wrote back to this man and said, "Thanks for the communication, but I think you're a scam. I'm blocking you." He must have been on the site when she sent it because he immediately wrote back, "What do you mean I'm a scam, we've met before."

She'd actually experienced this man in real life, flesh and blood had met this man, and because of her TGTBT Syndrome she couldn't have what was right in front of her. He was too good to be true.

We do this more often than you might think. We put our desires out there to the Universe, we ask for it, we pray for it every night, and then when the thing we asked for shows up we resist it and tell ourselves it can't possibly be real.

Let's say you went out to eat and ordered your dinner being very clear you would like a house salad with no tomatoes and the dressing on the side, Brussels sprouts instead of green beans and the halibut cooked medium-rare. When the waiter returns and presents your meal exactly as you requested it you don't sit there and go, "Wait a minute. This is exactly what I ordered. Is this some kind of scam? I don't trust this food." You would never ever do that, would you?

Usually what leads to TGTBT Syndrome is some form of feeling you aren't good enough to deserve what you desire. My understanding is that God is pretty busy and doesn't have time to be presenting you, me, and the other seven billion people on this planet with things we are not worthy of receiving. So what if instead of assuming you aren't deserving of what comes your way, you decided whenever something is presented to you, a romantic partner, a dream job, an expertly prepared meal that your friend insists on paying for, it means God has decided you are worthy of receiving it? And you simply say "thank you!"

When you do this you cure yourself of TGTBT Syndrome. No more questioning how or why or what you did to deserve it, simply welcome the fact that if it is there you must deserve it.

Oh and regarding the idea that we can believe the Universe has our back for little things but not being as confident the same is true for bigger things, the truth is to the Universe everything is the same in size. There are no "big things" versus "small things" to the Universe. We are the ones cutting ourselves off from Universal support once we hit our threshold of receptivity, our TGTBT Syndrome gets activated, and we go into resistance.

Everything we desire is equal in size to the Universe. Remember, this is the power which created everything that is, so there's really no point in persisting in the belief there is a limit in the Universe's ability to provide for you.

In the movie "The Empire Strikes Back" there is a scene where Yoda is encouraging Luke to use The Force to extract his X-wing Starfighter from where it is stuck in the swamp.

Luke sees the Starfighter sinking and says, *"We'll never get it out now."*

Yoda: *So certain are you? Always with you it cannot be done. Do you hear nothing that I say?*

Luke: *Master, moving stones around is one thing. This is totally different.*

Yoda: *No! No different. Only different in your mind. You must unlearn what you have learned.*

Luke: *Alright, I'll give it a try.*

Yoda: *No! Try not! Do or do not. There is no try.*

So Luke gives it a go. At first he is making progress and it looks promising, but then the ship sinks back into the swamp and he is defeated. He throws himself down in front of Yoda and says, *"I can't. It's too big."*

Yoda replies, *"Size matters not."* (I never realized it was Yoda who cleared this up for everyone. :-P)

Luke sulks off saying *"You want the impossible."*

Here is the part we forget about, after Yoda proceeds to use The Force and lifts the Starfighter out of the swamp, Luke comes to him and says:

Luke: *"I don't, I don't believe it."*

And Yoda responds: *"That is why you fail."*

Not believing is resistance to believing. This resistance is what keeps us from experiencing all that's available to us in the moment.

ACTION STEP TWO

Resisting resistance would simply be adding another layer to the problem, so to remedy this I developed a powerful visualization that allows my clients to envision releasing their resistance without having to resist it to do so.

(So that I may guide you through releasing your resistance I invite you to download a short video demonstration of this visualization at followyouryes.com/release.)

Resistance is experienced as fear; the degree of fear equates to the strength of Resistance. Therefore the more fear we feel about a specific enterprise, the more certain we can be that that enterprise is important to us and to the growth of our soul.

That's why we feel so much Resistance.

If it meant nothing to us, there'd be no Resistance.

- Steven Pressfield[33]

Believing is how we open the door to possibilities and tap into the divine guidance, support and power that is available to all of us. I assure you dropping your resistance and being open to possibilities is always a happier place to be than sitting in disbelief and resistance.

The less resistance you have, the easier it is to recognize and follow your YES.

Nobody ever died of discomfort, yet living in the
name of comfort has killed more ideas, more opportunities,
more actions and more growth than everything else combined.
- T. Harv Eker[34]

— 15 —

Your Comfort Zone and Your YES

Your comfort zone is a psychological state in which things feel familiar to you and you are at ease and (perceive you are) in control of your environment. The primary job of our brain is to make sure we survive, in other words, don't die. For this reason our brain likes things which are familiar, things we've experienced before and survived. Our brains perceive the familiar as safe. It has nothing to do with happiness or joy or fulfillment. For those of us who desire something different from life than what we are currently experiencing, perhaps more success, love or prosperity, our comfort zone is not very comfortable.

Many of your YESES fit easily within your comfort zone. These YESES encourage you to continue something you are already doing. Other YESES will not fit in your comfort zone because they require you to do something new or different.

Fear not. Your YES is always guiding you towards your highest good.

It may not always seem like the most direct path, but I promise you this is where your YES is leading you. It's also leading you toward a more expansive comfort zone. Writing this book was definitely unfamiliar for me as I have never written a book before. In fact, I used to say I would never write a book because I don't like writing. This was my brain resisting my heart. My brain was saying, "Ken, you've never written a book before. This is not familiar. We don't know if it's safe. What if people laugh at you? What if they say you're a fraud? We don't know if you can survive writing a book. You better stay here and stay safe by doing what you've been doing and not writing one."

I know the idea of writing a book being dangerous may sound ridiculous, but to your brain it doesn't. Unless I was Stephen King or James Patterson or Margaret Atwood or someone else for whom writing a book is a familiar thing my brain is going to see an unfamiliar action or activity as unsafe. Yours will too.

Alex Honnold is an American rock climber best known for his free solo ascents of big walls. This means he climbs without any ropes or protection of any kind. There is zero room for error when free soloing, which is why most of the world's top rock climbers don't do it. One mistake and you fall to your death. For years climbing El Capitan, a 3,000-foot granite wall in Yosemite National Park, was Alex's YES, but it was too scary. As he stated in the Academy Award winning documentary *Free Solo*[35]: "I've thought about El Cap for years. I've always wanted to [free solo climb it] but been like, that's too scary."

He goes on to say (in 2016): "I've thought about this since 2009. Each year since 2009 I've been like this is the year I climb it, and then I'm like this isn't the year. This is fucked. But the thing is I'll never be content unless I at least put in the effort."

So, Alex kept studying the route he'd climb, getting more and more familiar with it until it wasn't "too scary" anymore. Here's how he explains it: "When people talk about trying to suppress your fear, I look at it a different way. I try to expand my comfort zone by practicing the moves over and over again. I work through the fear until it's just not scary anymore."

Your YES is not always something you act on immediately, but that doesn't mean it is not still guiding you. Like Alex with the climb of El Cap, which he completed in June of 2017, or me writing this book.

Here's the thing ... we've made the idea of transforming your comfort zone scary by presenting it as "you have to get out of your comfort zone." That sounds like you're being cast out into the wilderness.

It's not really so much about getting out of your comfort zone. It's about expanding it. It's about making the space bigger, so now you have more space to play. This allows your comfort zone to fill with things that support you in being your best. When working with my clients on expanding their comfort zone I take them through a simple meditative exercise that is fast, effective and works every time.

(If you are interested in having me walk you through this same exercise you can download this guided meditation at followyouryes.com/comfort.)[36]

By transforming your so called comfort zone, which more accurately should be called your "Familiar but Frustrating Zone," and shifting it into a true comfort zone that is fun and exciting and actually assists you in loving your life, you are coming home.

Sometimes the place you are used to is not the place you belong.

- from the film *The Queen of Katwe*[37]

Following your YES transforms your comfort zone from being filled with limiting subconscious habits of survival into a place of conscious choices that support you in blooming, thriving, and living with joy in your heart.

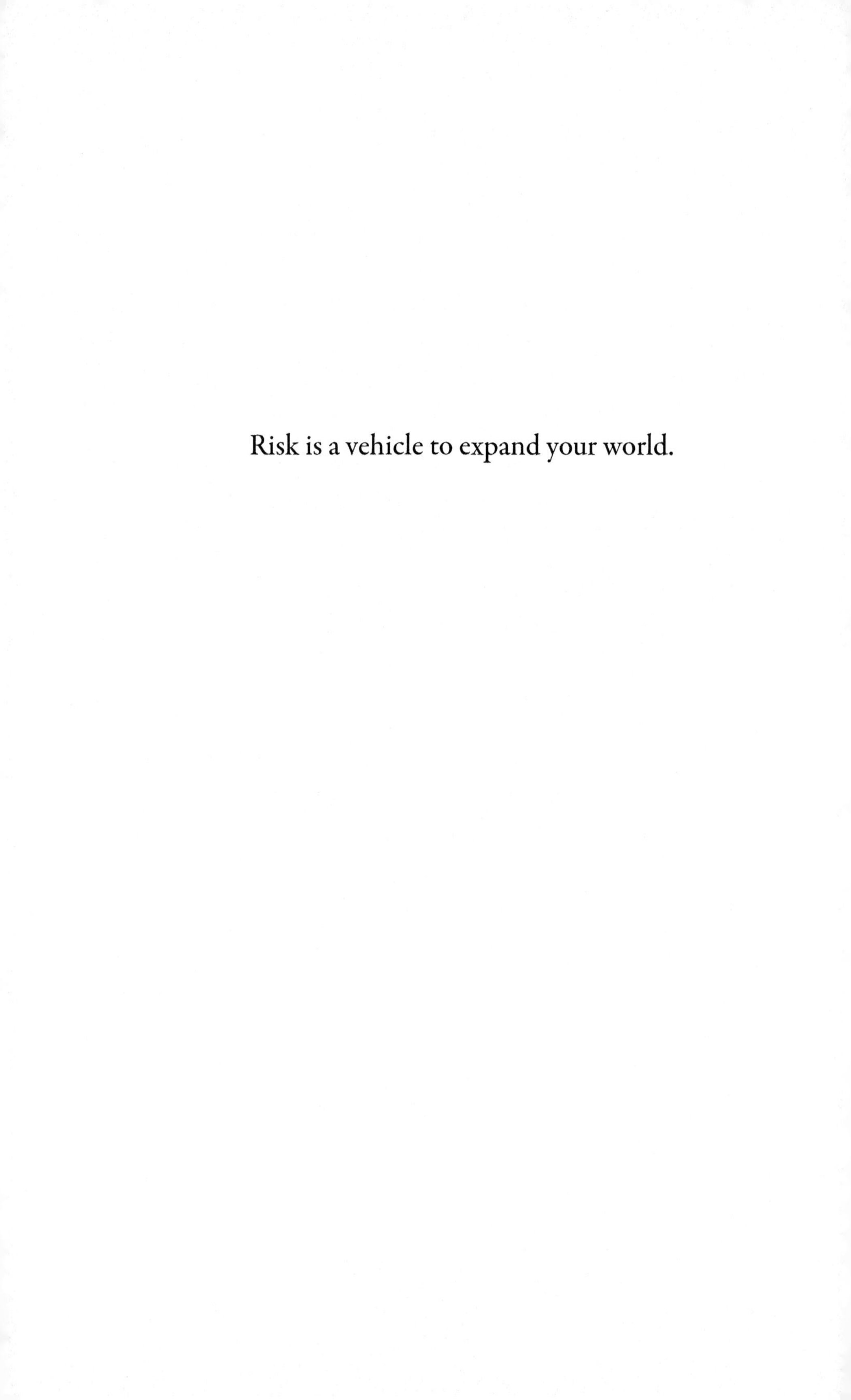

Risk is a vehicle to expand your world.

— 16 —

Risk and Your YES

I will warn you that just because something is your YES, it doesn't mean it won't feel risky sometimes.

Risk simply means there is a possibility something unpleasant or unwelcome could happen. Which is pretty much always a possibility.

If we want to progress in our lives, we have to embrace risk.

Many of us have been taught our whole lives to avoid risk at all costs. Avoiding risk is how we get smaller and smaller and smaller. What I invite you to open up to is the possibility that risk is a vehicle to expand your world.

Only those who will risk going too far can
possibly find out how far one can go.

- T.S. Eliot[38]

When you think about it, love could easily be spelled R-I-S-K. Success could be spelled R-I-S-K. Growth could be spelled R-I-S-K.

What I'm talking about is the *feeling* of love, growth, success and pretty much everything else we aspire to in life.

If you want to feel love, it's going to take risking being yourself and being seen so you can be appreciated for who you truly are.

If you want to feel successful it's going to require risk: trying new things, expanding and learning.

If you want to feel growth it requires risk. The risk of failing.

It doesn't take any risk to accomplish nothing. I'm not talking about the *act* of love or growth or success. I'm talking about experiencing the *feeling* of these things. And that's what life's all about ... feelings and feeling alive!

My voice teacher Sarah, who I mentioned earlier, used to say, "I don't care if you've got the words right. I don't care if you hit all the notes perfectly. Just don't stop singing. Bring it strong and wrong. Bring yourself to the performance, whether you're nailing it exactly as it was written, or not."

I used to think this advice was crazy. I didn't want to look stupid and fail at performing a song in front of the class. Even if they were my friends. That was too risky and embarrassing to fathom.

Then I heard a famous performance by the "First Lady of Song" Ella Fitzgerald and what Sarah was saying became clear to me in a heartbeat.

The performance I'm talking about was recorded live in Berlin, Germany in 1960. This particular performance is of the song "Mack the Knife,"[39] and on the recording you hear her introduce the song by saying, "We hope we remember all the words."

Now imagine you are a world class performer, and you're actually not sure you know all the words to the song you're about to perform. Is that a risk? Uh huh.

There's nothing safe about standing in front of a paying audience and telling them you may not know the song you are about to sing. Plus the performance was being recorded to make a new album. Another huge risk, and yet she did it.

By the way - Ella actually did forget the words. It is quite amazing to hear someone of her stature singing "Oh what's the next chorus?" because she forgot the lyrics to the song she is performing.

The question which naturally comes to mind when we learn of someone taking a risk like this is "Was it worth it?" That's always what we want to know, don't we? We can justify a risk if the outcome is worth it.

Well let's see. Today, more than 60 years after she recorded this album, Ella's version of "Mack the Knife" as she sang it that night in Berlin (when she forgot the words), is the most popular version ever recorded, other than the original. The album they recorded that night went on to win two Grammy Awards. Sounds like it was worth the risk, wouldn't you say?

Now not everybody is going to have such a big reward available to them from the risks they take, but if we don't take the risks, we prevent ourselves from having the opportunity to grow and reap the rewards that are available.

The day came when the risk to remain tight in a bud
was more painful than the risk it took to blossom.

- Anais Nin[40]

Clearly risks vary in size and consequences. This is why we have to take calculated risks. Much like with investments. A wise investor is aware of the risk and identifies how much they are willing to risk - potentially lose - as the consequence of taking that risk if things go poorly.

Ella Fitzgerald had to decide if trying to sing a song she might not remember the words to was worth the risk. She just as easily could have had the audience start booing her, the record company charge her for ruining the new album, found herself being ridiculed in the press, and concert dates cancelled. She went in with her eyes wide open that there was the possibility she would forget and bad things could come as a result, but she trusted her YES to guide her and did it anyway. Even when her fear of forgetting the words came to fruition, she still reaped the rewards of an award-winning hit album.

Learning we can overcome and recover from challenges actually strengthens us, making it easier to face other fears, and take additional risks.

There is always a reward associated with taking risks, it just may not be the one we first expect.

The more you follow your YES, the more comfortable you get with risk. Soon things don't feel as risky because you're starting to trust your abilities. You are building your risk-embracing muscles which leads to greater and greater rewards.

The more you follow your YES the less worry, doubt and fear you feel because you've learned that following YES leads you to joy and passion and satisfaction.

Choosing to follow your YES is the difference between a totally enhanced personal life, professional life, family life, and love life, or more of the same old, same old.

Your YES is your shortcut to happiness, prosperity and love. Your YES is the gateway through which you stop waiting, confidently make decisions, and enjoy life again.

Which do you prefer? Do you want to take the shortcut or stay on the long, circuitous route you've been traveling? The choice is yours.

FOLLOW YOUR YES FORMULA

STEP ONE
Look with Different Eyes

STEP TWO
Release Resistance

ACTION STEP - Go to followyouryes.com/release to access a short video demonstration of how to release your resistance without having to resist it to do so. The less resistance you have, the easier it is to recognize and follow your YES.

Your YES is always guiding you towards your highest good and a more expansive comfort zone. Receive access to a simple meditative exercise to expand your comfort zone at followyouryes.com/comfort.

The more you follow your YES the less worry, doubt and fear you feel because you've learned that following your YES leads you to joy and passion and satisfaction.

STEP THREE
Two Simple Questions

(You can download a printable version of the complete formula cheat sheet at followyouryes.com/cheatsheet)

STEP THREE

TWO SIMPLE QUESTIONS

As humans we love to ask *why*.

- Why did they stand me up?
- Why didn't they call when they said they would?
- Why did they fire me?
- Why didn't they tell me they weren't happy with my performance?

So why do we ask why? Often it has to do with what is called cognitive dissonance which simply means that something gets out of alignment with what you believe to be true. You have a belief like: good things should happen to good people because life is fair. Someone ghosting you, which you find to be inconceivably rude and unfair, or getting fired even though you do a good job creates a lack of alignment between your belief and what you are experiencing — dissonance. In order to reconcile these things, we ask "Why did that happen?"

Clearly *why* has its role, but there are other attributes we assign to *why* that are inaccurate.

Where we get off course with why is in believing that knowing *why* will set us free and allow us to move forward. It won't. The continual quest for *why* is a distraction that keeps us from moving forward. It delays progress and it leads to a deferred life. For example: "I feel like I can't move on until

I know why they broke up with me" is a common statement I've heard from my relationship clients over the years.

I was speaking with a client last week, and we uncovered two key limiting beliefs were holding her back in her dating and relationship life. One was the fear of physical closeness and the other was the fear she will be taken advantage of emotionally and financially by a partner if she opens herself to him.

These were life-changing revelations. It was a very powerful moment for her. Guess what she said next? "Maybe I should work with a psychotherapist to figure out *why* I have these blocks."

Looking for *why* is a very natural reaction, but what you have to understand is this is your reptilian brain putting the brakes on your progress. *Why* is a distraction from progress. Think about it. When you get sick will knowing why you got sick help you get well? No!

What moves you forward are 1) recognizing your current condition, where you are now, "I'm sick," and 2) taking action to find a solution that leads to where you want to be, like getting some rest, taking medicine or consulting a doctor. Let's say you go to the doctor. Does your doctor ask why you got sick before treating you? NO. They assess your condition and treat you accordingly. No *why* is needed.

Another enticement of the distraction of *why* is the idea that if we just know why something happened this will prevent it from happening again. This is not true either. Let's say you got a flat tire. Does knowing a nail punctured your tire prevent you from getting another flat? No. The problem here is twofold: 1) The only way to prevents future flats with this information is if you drive your car very slowly from now on so you can scour the road for nails and avoid them. It is very unlikely you will do this; 2) more things than just nails can cause a flat tire like glass and wire and sharp rocks etc. So even if you can avoid every nail from now on that does not keep you from getting a flat.

On top of this, when you seek out *why* so you can avoid something, you are now focusing on what you don't want. This is watering the weeds.

Focusing on *why* causes your world to get smaller, scarier and more limited.

When you make a mistake, don't look back at it long.
Take the reason of the thing into your mind and then look forward.
Mistakes are lessons of wisdom. The past cannot be changed.
The future is yet in your power.

- Hugh White[41]

What we do have the opportunity to gain from looking into the past is clarity. We can recognize the gifts we received, such as noticing you failed to speak up for yourself at work and let your boss walk all over you and how it didn't work for you. Leave the rest behind and move forward with this knowledge and awareness. From now on, when you feel like you're about to stay quiet yet again and allow yourself to be disrespected in any situation, you check in and remember you know how that ends. You already received that gift. You don't need to repeat this and pay the price for it all over again.

Past experiences are like birthday presents. When someone hands us a birthday present and it's all wrapped up in pretty paper with a ribbon and a bow on it, we call this the gift. Yet as soon as we remove the bow and the ribbon, tear off the wrapping paper and open the box we find the gift was what was inside. As soon as we recognize the gift was inside, the bow and the ribbon and the wrapping paper and the box instantly transform from being seen as the gift to being the trash and we release them.

The gift is always what's inside, not the outside packaging. Recognize the gift that was inside the experience and release all the rest, just like you do with the ribbon, the bow and the wrapping paper.

ACTION STEP THREE

Instead of asking why did something happen or why did they do this or say that, ask these two simple questions: "Where am I now?" and "Where do I want to be?" These are the questions that are relevant for progress. This is how you find your YES that you are meant to follow in this moment.

Let's say you are dating someone and they ghost you. This sucks! But instead of putting your energy into, "*Why* did they do this? I thought we were getting along great."

I propose you ask, "Where am I now?" (Sad, angry, possibly broken hearted.)

Then ask yourself: "Where or what do I want to be?" (Happy, empowered, in love.)

The longest route to where you want to be is always through *why* because it stops you from moving forward. Again, your reptilian brain is about survival and it hates risk and taking new approaches to things.

When you delve into why something happens, it keeps you occupied so you don't take risks or try something new.

Why keeps you stuck in the past. There is no progress in the past because you can't change it and you can't create anything from there. The only place you can create is the present.

Why is a distraction we've gotten hooked on as a culture. Be mindful of what you are counting on *why* doing for you. If you are looking to *why* to reconcile some dissonance between what you believe and what you have experienced, then *why* is a great tool. In all other situations I recommend you ask yourself, "Where am I now?" and "Where do I want to be?" When you genuinely pay attention to the answers you receive to these questions, you typically find the *why* about your past is not really essential to your future.

The lessons you bring forward from the past are what support you in taking your next step and creating your future now. Your next step is your YES, and as we've discussed throughout this book, your mission is to simply focus on going from YES to YES to YES to YES.

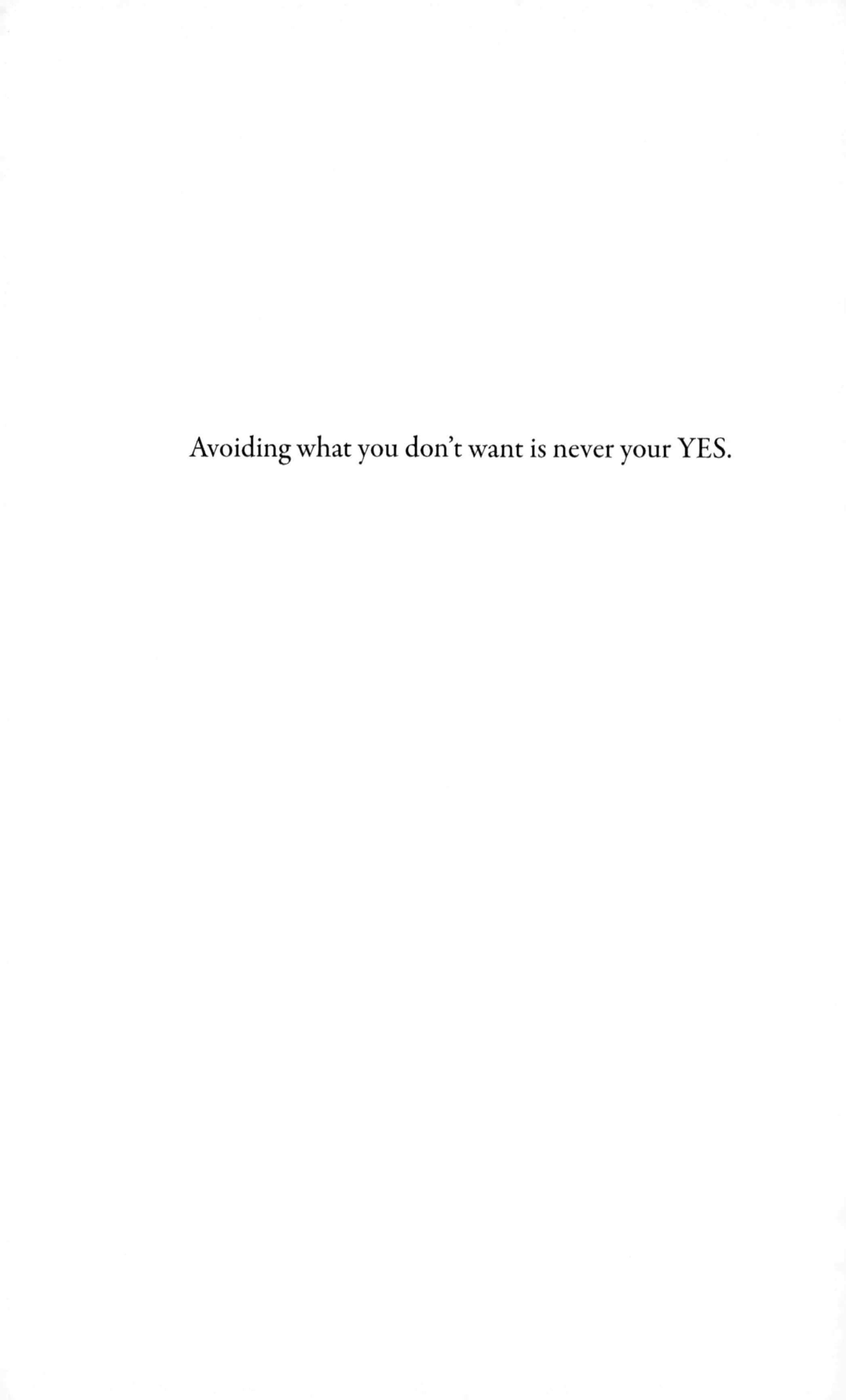

Avoiding what you don't want is never your YES.

— 17 —

Focus on What You DO Want

We all have an incredibly effective tool for manifesting the life we want. It is your secret weapon, but sadly, most people don't know they have it, and those that do often misuse it. It is called the Reticular Activating System (RAS) and it's a bundle of nerves at your brainstem that takes what you focus on and creates a filter for it. It filters the world through the parameters you give it. Whenever you think about or focus on something specific and suddenly you see it everywhere you look, this is your RAS in action. You are thinking about having a baby and suddenly it seems like there are pregnant women and babies everywhere you look. Or you learn a new word and then start hearing it everywhere.

Not long ago I purchased a Saab automobile. Now Saab stopped making cars over 10 years ago so you don't see many on the road anymore, but I always liked them and found one that had been owned by a man who used to work for Saab and babied this car, so it was in mint condition. I went to pick up the car and he said to me. "You don't see many of these anymore. I hope you enjoy it as much as I did." And wouldn't you know it, on the five-mile drive back home I must have seen a half dozen Saabs on the road. I even passed a repair shop cleverly named East of Sweden, that specialized in only Swedish cars — Saabs and Volvos — less than a mile from my house. Those cars and that repair shop had been there all along, but up until I put my attention on Saabs I didn't notice them. Once I focused on Saabs all sorts of things Saab-related came into focus. My RAS literally sorted out what I was now focused on from all the other things occupying my world and presented them to me.

If you've ever been tempted to conclude things like, all the single people in my area are too young or all the companies who are hiring in my industry don't pay enough, or all the prospective customers I meet are just bargain shopping and don't care about quality, these are examples of your RAS in action helping you spot the things you don't want. It works both ways. Whether what you focus on is what you do want or what you don't want, your RAS will bring them front and center for you.

Avoiding what you don't want is never your YES. And here's why -

The Divine always moves you towards something,
never away from something.

Answer this question for yourself: In your day-to-day choices are you usually moving towards what you do want or away from what you don't want? Focusing on what we don't want is a completely natural approach —it's called survival. You are trying to avoid the pain you experienced in previous relationships, the disrespect you endured when you felt not listened to, or the embarrassment you felt when someone ridiculed you. So you make a mental list: Here are the things I definitely don't want, and that's what you're feeding your Reticular Activating System.

As much as you may want it to, moving away from what you don't want does not automatically move you towards what you do want. Instead, it typically leads you to more stuff you don't want.

This is the result of using your Reticular Activator to spot what you DON'T want instead of using it to move towards what you DO want. It also guarantees your route to your Mr./Mrs. Right or a rewarding career or finding the home of your dreams etc. will be the longest one possible. Imagine if the GPS in your car worked like this. You get in the car and enter your intended destination and then the GPS starts telling you all the ways you DON'T want to go to get there. "Don't take highway 7. Don't take Main Street. Don't turn left. Don't back up." And so on.

If this is how GPS worked, how long do you think it will take to reach your destination? For that matter how long would it take you to even get out of your driveway if you have to list off all the ways not to get there first?

Stop wasting precious energy on what you do not want.
Focus that energy on creating the life you do want.
This is not only a gift to offer yourself, but all those in your orbit.
By your rising above you lift others higher with
your positive attitude and inspiring example.

- Karen Salmansohn[42]

Focus on what you do want, feed it, and recognizing your YES will become easier because the Divine is always guiding you towards things, not away from them. When you recognize something as being a thing you don't want, a NO, don't spend a lot of time dwelling on it. Dwelling on it is like watering the weeds in your garden and then wondering why the weeds grow so much faster than your rose does. There is no benefit to putting your energy into the things you don't want. Instead, simply recognize it for what it is, something that doesn't serve you, and then decide what you want to replace it with.

BONUS ACTION STEP

Here's a great exercise[43] to help you use your awareness about what you *don't* want as a means of identifying what you *do* want, so you can feed that into your Reticular Activating System instead. Don't underestimate the power of this simple exercise. Most people who I take through this exercise get a HUGE "Ah-Ha" from it, so be ready.

Take out a piece of paper and divide it into three columns and at the top of the left column write the word Complaint like this:

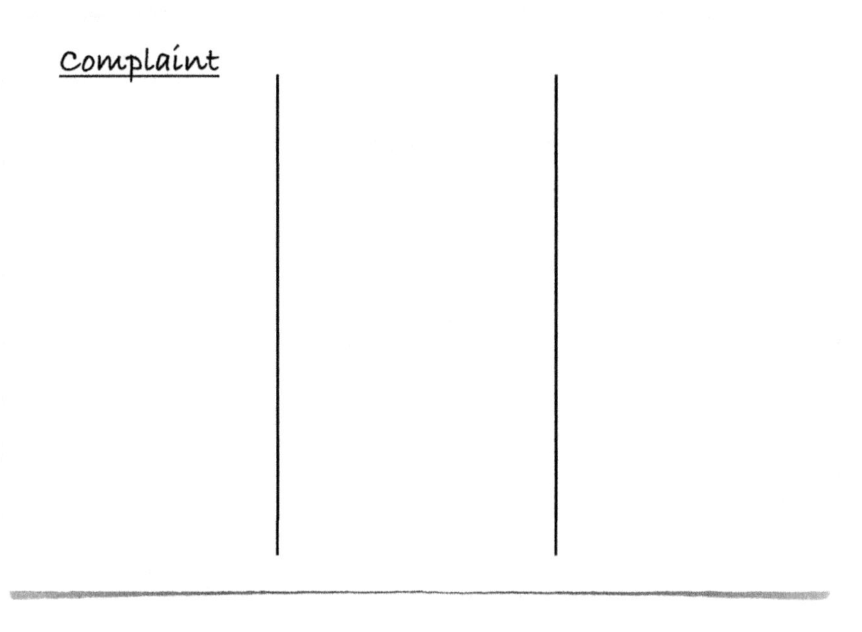

Now list a few things you complain about, in your relationships, your work, or your day-to-day life. This could be a complaint you said out loud or one you just complained about in your head. They all count as complaints.

No one else will see your list so just jot down a word or two so you know what it is.

- Always late.
- Never pick up socks.
- Interrupt you when you're talking.
- Not appreciated for the work you do.

Whatever it is for you, write them down. Take a couple of minutes right now to list at least three to four complaints that are most top of mind for you right now. You can always come back and add more later.

In the center column, write down the word Wanted. What do you want instead of what you got?

This thing you wanted is what matters to you.

Example: if you complained someone was always late then punctuality may be what matters to you.

Take a couple of minutes to fill this section in now. When you're done your page will now look something like this:

Complaint	Wanted	
Always late	Punctual	
Slob	Neat	
Interrupt you	Listens	
Not appreciated	Recognition	

On the left are complaints, in the center is what you wanted instead of what you got and the right column is empty.

Be aware the things you complain about will always reveal some type of value you have that has been dishonored. So, if you complained about punctuality then you probably value the effective use of your time and since they were always late, this value was dishonored. See it?

Complaints always reveal what is important to you, so they are a great way to identify what you value.

Clearly, we're not done yet since we have one more column to fill in. We want to identify the feelings associated with the things you have listed because this is what we are going to feed into your Reticular Activating System. At the top of the right-hand column write Provides/Feel.

Now, list how you feel when you receive the things you listed in the center "Wanted" column. If you haven't experienced this yet then write down how you imagine you would feel when you receive this thing.

In our example, what does someone being punctual provide for you? What is the feeling you experience from having them be punctual? How does it make you feel? Safe, special, valued, a priority, respected, like you can trust them, etc. Of course, you will apply this to whatever you have written in your center column. Whatever it is for you, write it next to each item in your list.

Know that whatever the feeling is for you it is completely valid. Remember feelings are unarguable.

Here are some questions to ask yourself to help determine what something will provide:

- How will this make you feel when you have what is in your center column?
- Who will you be able to be or want to be?
- What will you be able to do or be willing to do?
- How will this change your life?
- How will this change your experience of the situation/person?

Take a couple minutes and fill this column in now.

Now your page looks something like this:

Complaint	Wanted	Provides/Feel
Always late	Punctual	Important/Respected
Slob	Neat	Safe/Clean
Interrupt you	Listens	Valued/A Contributor
Not appreciated	Recognition	Significant/ Successful

These items in the right hand column—what it provides for you—are the feelings you are looking for. These are the feelings you want to feed into your Reticular Activating System so it can show them to you. Do you see how this ties in with the first step in the formula of Looking with Different Eyes? You are looking for the feeling that is your YES.

For now all you need to do with the feelings you identified is to feel into them. If you are looking to feel important/respected then take a couple of minutes and let that feeling wash over you and fill you up. Literally set a timer and give yourself two minutes to do this.

A simple way to do this is to assign a color to the feeling you are looking to experience. Any color you pick will work. Say you assign the color gold to feeling important/respected. Close your eyes and imagine the color gold filling you in and feel what that feels like to you. There is no wrong answer. Just relax and feel it right here in present time. When your two minute timer goes off, open your eyes and proceed to the next chapter. Well done!

— 18 —

Stop Watering the Weeds

Focusing on what you do want is a muscle, and we all have this muscle. Unfortunately, since many of us haven't been using this muscle very much, it has become weak. Instead, we have developed very strong survival muscles by focusing on what we don't want. We have been programmed to endure. This is like becoming an expert at treading water but never developing the ability to swim and move in the direction of our choosing. We just float around at the whim of the tide and the waves.

We've all heard the adage: Hope for the best, plan for the worst. This may sound like wise advice. After all, you never know when things can go sideways so you had best be prepared. I get it, but let me ask you something ... when you are hoping for the best but planning for the worst, where is most of your energy going? It's going to the things you don't want, the worst-case scenarios, right? You are literally focusing on what you don't want. You are watering the weeds instead of your rose.

When you approach life this way, is it possible you will be so focused on preparing for the worst that you will see things as going badly and miss out on the good stuff?

An experience my former housemate Suzanne had is a textbook illustration of this.

Suzanne was excitedly planning for her first overnight camping trip in Colorado. She had lived all over the world, but had never camped anywhere overnight before and the idea of sleeping in a tent outside had her all jazzed up.

She was going as part of a group trip organized by a very experienced and professional outdoor activities group. And even though they were being led by veteran guides she wasn't taking any chances. So off to the local sporting goods store she went to equip herself with everything she could possibly need for any circumstances that may arise. The trip organizers had provided a comprehensive list of what to bring and Suzanne planned to have everything on the list and then some when she hit the trail.

As she said, "I always hope for the best but plan for the worst. That's what my Mom taught me." I can promise you when Suzanne left for her trip she had all her "plans for the worst" in place and more than enough supplies to execute them including the knowledge she had gained from 4 different books on backpacking.

Fast forward two days to when she returned looking spent, disappointed and dejected. I tentatively asked how it went and she let me know in no uncertain terms it was the worst trip ever. The guides were awful. The weather was awful, it was windy and cold. Her pack was super heavy and she got blisters from her new hiking boots. The list of disasters that made up her trip was extensive.

I was sad for her, because she had been so excited about camping and this becoming her new passion, but it was clear this was not going to be the case. Later in the week I heard from my friend Jen. It turned out Jen was on the same camping trip as Suzanne was, so I asked her how it went. She said it was great. One of the best led trips she had ever been on.

When I shared with her what Suzanne had said she replied: "I'm not surprised. Suzanne was so focused on all the things that could go wrong that for her they did."

First, Suzanne's backpack was at least double the size of everyone else's and when the lead guide suggested she leave some of it in the car since they were only going to be gone for one night, Suzanne refused insisting she needed all of it "just in case." Then after they set up camp, the guide got a report that a storm was coming in, so he recommended everyone move their tent into the trees for more protection. But Suzanne did not want to move. She had been so busy collecting all her supplies for the various bad scenarios that might happen that she never took the time to practice setting up her new tent before the trip. As a result, she had an awful time setting it up and did not want to break it down and have to put it back up in the trees. So she stayed put in the meadow. Other campers offered to help her move her tent, but she insisted she would be fine where she was and if it was such a terrible place to be the guide would have never had them set their tents up there in the first place.

Well, you can probably guess what happened next. The storm did roll in with high winds and cold slashing rain which came down in sheets. The next morning when Suzanne trudged down to the main campfire to get some coffee and breakfast, she looked like she hadn't slept a wink.

So how did Suzanne and Jen go on the exact same trip with the exact same guides in the exact same weather and have such different experiences?

Suzanne was focused on what could go wrong and put her energy into watering the weeds and guess what grew? Meanwhile, Jen was focused on having a good time, trusting the guides and enjoying the outdoors. She manifested those things by watering the flowers of what she wanted to grow.

Whatever you put your energy into you will experience.

With the Reticular Activating System we talked about earlier, what you put in, no matter if it is positive or negative, will come back multiplied. So when you feed it what you don't want, you end up seeing disappointments all around you. Chances are if someone gave you the advice to hope for the best but plan for the worst, as Suzanne's mother did, they didn't know about the Reticular Activating System. They didn't know our RAS is always working whether we are consciously feeding it our goals and desires or our fears and concerns.

It is easier to get pulled by a positive future than to get pushed by things we are trying to get away from.

- Gay Hendricks[44]

You are a rose, so focus on blooming and stop watering the weeds, the fears of the future and the heartaches and disappointments of the past. When you focus on what you do want and then plant it, water it, and nurture it you more easily recognize the YESES that support you in blooming and living your best life.

— 19 —

Driving Blindfolded

One of the crucial elements of becoming skilled at following your YES is being mindful of whether what you feel is your YES is about advancement or avoidance. Are you looking where you want to go, or are you looking to avoid that which you fear? It's easy to convince ourselves that our YES is guiding us to avoid something we fear, like public speaking, but this is never the case. Your YES is about what supports you in blooming. So if public speaking does not support you in blooming, your YES will guide you towards something that does. No one has ever bloomed by avoiding.

Blooming is the opposite of avoiding.

Your fears will never move you forward to your goals. Fear moves you towards low-risk, low-reward options, and back to familiar disappointing territory while you try to deny you want to be somewhere else. A great demonstration of the benefits of following our guidance instead of our fears takes place at high performance driving schools where they teach people how to drive race cars. They do an exercise where a series of pylons are set up and the student drives through the course with the instructor sitting next to them letting them know when to "turn left, turn right, turn left" so they don't hit the cones. A surprising thing happens when they do this. Without fail the student will hit one or more of the pylons even though the instructor is telling them exactly when to turn so they don't hit anything. Then they go back and start the course over, only this time the driver is blindfolded. That's right, the person driving can't see a thing. Again, the instructor is letting them know when to *"turn left, turn right, turn left"* and the student will sail through the course without hitting a single pylon.

How can this be?

It's because we tend to focus on our fears instead of our goals. We focus on the pylons we don't want to hit, instead of the clear path between the pylons.

I learned this lesson by riding my bike. Whenever I would see a pothole in the road in front of me I'd focus on it and think, *I don't want to hit that. I could get a flat if I hit it. I hate changing flats on the side of the road. Please don't let me hit the pothole.* And then I would ride smack into the pothole every time.

It took me a while to get this into my bones, where I didn't just know what to do - focus on the smooth road - but I actually applied what I knew. What finally got me to apply what I knew happened on a Sunday morning when I was out on my first bike ride since dislocating my shoulder. I was super excited to be able to ride again and headed out on a beautiful morning to spin the pedals and ride a few miles. I had been riding about 10 minutes when I saw a dark spot in the road ahead and assumed it was a pothole. Immediately all my focus went to this pothole - *I don't want to hit that. I could get a flat if I hit it. That would ruin my first ride in months. Please don't let me hit the pothole.*

Then BAM! Not only did I hit the dark spot in the road which I was desperately focused on avoiding, but it wasn't a pothole at all. It was a pile of cement that had fallen onto the road and hardened. It was like riding into a big rock that had been glued to the asphalt. My bike flipped up and everything went into slow motion. As I went flying over the handlebars heading towards a very hard impact with the road I literally yelled out loud, "You've got to be #@!%ing kidding me!!!" because I knew I was about to re-dislocate the same shoulder I had just recovered from, and that's exactly what I did.

A couple days after getting out of the hospital I went back to the site of the accident to retrieve my bicycle from the friendly people who, as I was being placed in the ambulance, offered to take care of my bike until I could come pick it up. I walked across the street to see what I had actually hit, and discovered the pile of concrete.

More important than identifying what I hit was noticing how much smooth road there was around the concrete. If I had just applied what I knew and focused on where I wanted to go instead of my fear of hitting a pothole, I would have had an uneventful and beautiful bike ride that day.

Nowadays when I see a pothole in the road in front of me, I look for the smooth road around it. I focus on where I do want to go instead of where I don't want to go and I ride smoothly around the pothole. I even thank the pothole for refocusing my attention on where I do want to go as I ride. I am certain there are no fewer potholes in the road now than there used to be. In fact there are probably more. But I don't worry about them because I am focused on where I do want to go, which is the smooth road. It was always there, I just had to choose it.

Do yourself a favor and learn from my mistake.

Don't wait until you crash, literally or metaphorically, before you redirect your focus to what you do want and where you do want to go. I promise you the longer you wait to make this shift the more pain you will experience.

INSIDER TIP

The act of avoiding something or someone is a huge energy suck. It is an all-encompassing activity which leaves you very little energy with which to create. Avoiding is a 24/7 activity. You can never stop avoiding for fear of this thing catching you. It's exhausting!

When we follow our YES which tells us exactly what direction to go to advance, we are able to get where we want to go without concerning ourselves with the things we used to avoid.

Listen to your own voice, your own soul,
too many people listen to the noise of
the world, instead of themselves.

Deep inside, you know what you want,
let no one decide that for you.

- Leon Brown[45]

— 20 —

Inner Authority

Chances are you are quite familiar with the many forms of external authority: bosses, parents, teachers, clergy, politicians, consultants, judges, people on TV, the internet and social media, etc. These authorities all have different impacts in our lives based on the conscious or sub-conscious agreements we have made with them.

Sadly, for many of us, we have lost contact with the most powerful authority in our life — our Inner Authority.

Authority is defined as the power or right to give orders and make decisions.

We often get programmed not to trust our Inner Authority. We become so uncomfortable listening to the answers we are receiving from inside that we ignore our divine guidance, our YES, and go looking for terrestrial guidance from others.

To follow your YES you have to reclaim your Inner Authority.

I had a client, named Karen, come to me and say she had just turned 70 and felt like she was still waiting for her life to start. Her entire life she had been asking others what they thought and looking for external approval. She had almost completely abandoned her Inner Authority. Midway through our work together she said to me, "Ken, I'm so happy to have realized that my life starts when I'm following my YES." I couldn't have been prouder. Here was a wonderful woman who had spent decades waiting for her life to start because she was waiting for someone else to start it for her, and now she had reconnected with her Inner Authority and wasn't waiting any longer. As Karen started following her YES she cleaned up her relationships with her siblings, reduced the amount of time she spent with people she used to think were her "best friends" that really weren't, and learned how to express her YESES in a way that was respectful of all involved.

Saying yes to yourself opens up opportunities that can take you anywhere. Having a mentor in your life who supports you in saying yes to you, is the key.

- Phyllis George[46]

When we stay in alignment where we're really paying attention to our YES, it's our shortcut to the life we've heard calling us from deep down inside. We're no longer filtering our choices and actions through everybody else's ideas of how we're supposed to live our life. We're living our life the way we're meant to be.

One of the most important teachers in my life was a woman named Mary Bell Nyman. She was the director of Psychic Horizons Center where I studied spirituality after moving to Boulder. Whenever I asked Mary Bell a question, no matter if I asked, "Am I doing this right?" or "How does this work?" Or "What should I do when ...?" she would reply with, "What do you think?" At first, this really irritated me. It seemed like an inappropriate thing for a teacher to do, but what I later realized was that she was helping me reconnect with my Inner Authority. She was really asking, what is your wisdom? What is your knowingness? What is the Divine telling you is the right answer for you? She was helping me to recognize I already had my answer, my YES.

We always have our own answer, it's simply a matter of trusting it, embracing it, and acting upon it. When you understand your YES is your divine guidance then you find comfort and ease in acting upon these things.

Mary Bell taught me our Inner Authority is where we find our answers. No one else has your answers. That is conditional. The best guidance we can ever find is from our connection with the Divine. When we are looking for someone else to approve our answers before we act on them, we are denying our Inner Authority, our divine guidance.

By the time I was a teacher at Psychic Horizons I was doing the same thing. When a woman in my class asked me a question and I said, "What do you think?" she got all agitated and shouted, "You're just like Mary Bell, you never answer the question you just give it back to me!"

I smiled and replied, "So what *do* you think?" and her answer flowed out.

Learning to trust our internal guidance is one of the most powerful skills you can ever develop. And I have a secret for you ... you already do it in some areas of your life, now it is time to expand it to all of your life.

Think about the last time you asked a waiter or a friend for advice about what to order at a restaurant and even though they may have raved about a certain dish and gone on and on about how it's the best thing ever, you still didn't order it. Or perhaps you read the reviews for a new movie and many of the reviewers hated it, but you still decided to go and loved it. Why? Your Inner Authority, your YES, overrode all the enthusiasm or bad reviews. You recognized their YES was not your YES. There is nothing wrong with asking for advice or counsel from another, but ultimately what is your YES is your decision. For you it might have been when you asked someone for directions on how to drive somewhere you had never been before and yet you didn't follow their directions. Now you may have consulted a map or GPS or some other resource, but your Inner Authority, your power to make decisions overruled the directions you were offered.

Unfortunately, most of us have given our authority away to other people, to society, to religion, to bosses, to family members, etc. Following your YES is reclaiming your Inner Authority, the divine guidance that is available to every one of us.

Just trust yourself, then you will know how to live.

- Johann Wolfgang von Goethe[47]

FOLLOW YOUR YES FORMULA

STEP ONE
Look with Different Eyes

STEP TWO
Release Resistance

STEP THREE
Two Simple Questions

ACTION STEP - To find your YES that you are meant to follow in this moment ask: "Where am I now?" and "Where do I want to be?" These are the questions that are relevant for progress.

BONUS ACTION STEP - Do the exercise that starts on page 135 to help you use your complaints about things you don't want as a means of identifying what you do want.

No matter what you put into your Reticular Activating System, no matter if it is positive or negative, it will come back multiplied. So be sure to feed it what you do want instead of what you don't want.

Your Inner Authority is where you find your answers. This is your connection with the Divine. No one else has your answers, trust yourself.

(You can download a printable version of the complete formula cheat sheet at followyouryes.com/cheatsheet)

What Next?

You now have the exact formula for following your YES that I've been using for years. These are the three steps you need to take to identify and then follow your YES.

In the beginning it's common to feel uncertain if you are doing it right or if you are actually following your YES or not. A great way to increase your certainty and quickly build your following your YES muscles is to start tracking the YESES you follow each day. There are many ways you can do this. One of the simplest is marking a calendar to show you followed a YES that day. I use something I call a Smile Journal because smiles are easy to recognize. Smiles are an ideal measuring stick because YESES tend to make you smile since you are acting in alignment with your truth. NOs and Maybes rarely if ever lead to a smile.

I've been writing in my Smile Journal every night since the idea came to me as my YES more than 20 years ago and the difference it's made in my sleep quality alone is amazing. Smiles are about what we DO have, right now, in present time. It is uncommon to smile about something you don't have or isn't working, and since we create more of whatever we focus on, let's focus on the smiles.

To follow this practice yourself select a special book or binder to be your Smile Journal. Then at the end of each day, as you get ready for bed, take 5 to 10 minutes and simply ask yourself: What YESES did I follow today? What made me smile? Start each entry with "I smiled today because … ." Then write out everything you come up with. If it made you smile or grin or lightened your heart in any way write it down. No judgement, even if it seems like a kind of strange thing to smile about write it down.

Here is the entry from my Smile Journal on 4/8/22 -

I smiled today because I took a nap. Reworking book and creating the formula chart. Big workout – felt strong. Great sessions with clients. Leftover pizza. Taking misdelivered mail to my neighbor. Pausing to listen to the red-winged blackbirds trill in my backyard. Carol asking me about singing together again. My enthusiastic YES. A gorgeous Spring day.

Your entries can be anything that was your YES that day. It doesn't have to be anything grand or flashy. Remember the vast majority of your YESES will be basic everyday things, not just giant life changing epiphanies. Perhaps for you it was:

- You completed a task you had been avoiding
- Making time to prepare a healthy meal
- You addressed an elephant in the room with someone
- Texting a friend to let them know you miss them
- Accepting an invitation to dinner
- Going to bed early

Keeping track of your YESES has many benefits. First it helps you stay motivated by providing visible evidence of your advancement as you document the YESES you follow each day. Don't worry about how many YESES you are following each day, instead stay focused on being consistent in following at least one YES every day.

Every day may not be good, but there is something good in every day.

- Alice Morse Earle[48]

Secondly, by doing this right before you go to bed you program your thoughts to be on smiles and successes, which is positive. This often leads to more restful sleep, plus when you fill your mind with happy thoughts your subconscious mind then works in the energy of things that make you smile while you are sleeping, instead of spending the night focused on your worries and fears. When you go to sleep thinking about the smiles you experienced that day, you take positive thoughts with you. How many of us can say we usually do that?

Plus documenting your YESES helps you keep your radar tuned to your YES instead of getting sucked in by the NOs and the Maybes that are circling around all the time. You will find yourself noticing each

YES you follow during the day and making a mental note to write them down in your journal.

As you build these muscles and the process of connecting with your YES becomes more second nature, feel free to make this formula your own. Find your own phrases or reminders to help you connect with your YES in the moment. When I first started I put Post-It notes around my house, on my computer, my car dash and my refrigerator door that simply read FYY. This was what I needed to remind myself to follow my YES. Try it yourself and see how it works for you. Nowadays those post-it notes are no longer needed. Today, whenever I notice I'm struggling with something (a sure sign I'm not following my YES) I pause for a moment and ask myself "What's my YES?" All the steps of the formula laid out for you here are automatic for me now, and as long as you stay consistent in this practice, it will be the same for you soon as well.

After a week of doing this practice every day I encourage you to take it up a notch. Much like in a fitness routine, once you've been doing the workout for a while it's time to add a few reps. Contrary to popular belief, it is repetition, not time that allows a conscious practice to become a sub-conscious one where it works pretty much on auto-pilot. So commit to doing this practice twice a day to accelerate your progress. The best way to remember to do this is to attach your practice to something you already do and would never skip. Brushing your teeth is a good one. Most people brush their teeth when they wake up and before going to bed, so declare you are going to do your Following your YES practice before you get to brush your teeth and you will never forget to do it.

After a week of two-a-days it's time to take your YES on the road. If you're like most people you've been doing this practice at home for the past couple weeks and are getting pretty comfortable with it. Now it's time to add an additional YES check-in when you are outside of your home. Use the same strategy you did when you stepped up to practice twice a day and attach checking in with your YES to something you do everyday outside of your house so you don't forget. You could do it before you get to check your email at work, before you get to open the mailbox and pick up your mail, or before you start your car.

You may find you have some resistance to taking your YES on the road. (If so, repeat STEP TWO of the formula - Release Resistance.) Doing this practice at home where no one can see you or knows you are doing it feels safe, but what if someone found out what you were up to? Or worse yet, what if the YES you get when you check in at work is "bad", like your YES is to not be at work. Notice this is what you don't want - to be at work. And you now know your YES is always nudging you towards something, so what is something you can do in the moment to address the recognition that you don't enjoy your job? Give yourself a relaxing breath, tip your head forward and look at your heart, then ask where are you now? And where do you want to be? Focus on the feelings.

Following your YES is proactively moving towards what you do want, not reactively going away from what you don't want. Your YES is never "bad." It is simply an indicator your life could be enhanced if you move in a certain direction.

The point of this step in the process is to help you feel safe connecting with your YES anywhere and anytime. Your YES can be like a best friend who is there for you anytime and anyplace when you develop this part of your practice.

Once you've consistently applied this formula and followed this practice every day for thirty days you'll be amazed how much more natural, simple, less scary, and less risky it feels to follow your YES. From here continue your practice and soon following your YES will be your default operating system.

Without commitment you'll never start. And more importantly without consistency you'll never finish.

- Denzel Washington[49]

If you are someone who knows you benefit from guidance and accountability then I invite you to join the YES-ify Your Life program where I guide you in simplifying, clarifying and amplifying your life. Go to followyouryes.com/program for all the details.

Know you're not limited by what you've read in this book. The possibilities available by following your YES are endless. This is one of the things following your YES does for you. It opens the door to possibilities, your possibilities. You're not limited by what others have done with their YES, you're free to do whatever you desire with yours.

— 21 —

Reward Follows Action

Reward always follows action. The action I am referring to is the action it takes to get in and stay in alignment with your truth, which is what following your YES is all about.

Fear not the path of truth for the lack of people walking on it.

- Robert F. Kennedy[50]

The challenge is the first actions we take rarely tend to show major results. Almost immediately when this happens, we start to rationalize how it wouldn't be so bad if we just stopped now. We start to convince ourselves we aren't really interested in the results. We romanticize the past and tell ourselves it really wasn't that bad.

Several years ago I was on a car camping trip and when I got to my campsite I set up my tent and then I pulled out the air mattress I had brought with me.

Full disclosure, I am not an avid camper. Sleeping on the cold, hard ground is not something I do often. I've done it, but if there's a more comfortable way, I prefer that. To this end I had purchased an air mattress.

My tent was a big family tent, big enough I could stand up in it and several people could comfortably sleep in sleeping bags. But since it was just me, I had purchased a queen size air mattress. I lay the mattress out and went looking for the pump to fill it up. Then I realized this mattress had a built-in pump you pushed on with your foot to fill the mattress. So, I started pushing up and down on this pump over and over again. Very quickly I was starting to sweat, getting winded, and seeing very little results. The results were so minimal, I wasn't sure anything was happening. I was starting to believe all the air I was pushing into the mattress was escaping when I released the pump. It looked to me like the mattress was never going to fill up.

Immediately I started trying to convince myself sleeping on the cold hard ground was not so bad. Who was I kidding? You weren't supposed to sleep on a nice comfortable air mattress when you were camping, I said to myself. Sleeping on the ground as part of the experience. Everyone else sleeps on the ground, why should I be different?

That's when my YES kicked in and said don't quit. You can have the comfortable air mattress experience you desire if you keep going. This is when I refocused on my vision of a comfortable night sleep on this plush air mattress, and I recommitted to my vision.

Now as this was going on other campers in the campgrounds were passing by my tent and they would look in as they heard the ruckus I was creating as I tried to pump up the air mattress. Many scornful looks were thrown my way. A few laughed. It was clear they were thinking that's not how you camp. Camping is not supposed to be a pleasure and comfort, it's about roughing it.

I could have adopted the idea that camping is about roughing it, and this may have been their YES, but it wasn't mine. I kept pumping.

After another 10 minutes of vigorous jumping up and down on the pump with sweat rolling off my face, I thought I saw some movement in the mattress. I may have just been delirious from all the effort, but I swore the mattress was starting to fill. Sure enough, the more I pumped the clearer it became that indeed I was making progress.

Then something amazing happened. All at once it appeared every single pump I made created a huge difference in how far the mattress was filling up. It seemed like each pump added another 10% and then 20% and before I knew it the mattress was full. I stood there catching my breath, sweating, and looking down at the mattress with great pride and excitement at what I had accomplished. That night I slept like a king on my plush comfortable air mattress in the middle of the woods. No, it didn't matter to me that others were choosing to sleep on the hard ground. What mattered was I chose and followed through on what served me best.

Neither I nor the other campers were right about their choice in a global sense. All that mattered was I follow through on what was right for me. I followed my YES.

Next time you start following your YES and get discouraged because you are not seeing results as quickly as you like, you can think of how ridiculous I looked jumping up and down to inflate my air mattress and how staying with it and continuing to follow my YES even when I couldn't see any results led to a blissful night's sleep. Better yet, take five minutes right now to think back and recall times in your own life when your actions led to rewards and let those be your touchstones.

The only place where success comes before work is in the dictionary.

- Vince Lombardi[51]

Commit to taking action and doing at least one thing today which will move you in the direction of the answer you got in STEP 3 when you asked yourself where you want to be. Allow your action to be a baby step if need be. The fact that you are following your YES and moving in the direction of your aspiration is more important than the size of the step you take.

Following your YES is not a passive lifestyle. Act, commit and recommit as often as you need to, and very soon you will be reaping the rewards.

— 22 —

Trust the System

Following your YES is a lot like ordering food at a restaurant. When you order food at a restaurant you trust the system. You don't follow the waiter into the kitchen to see if they know what they're doing and tell them how to prepare your meal. You trust the system. You have zero doubt the meal you just ordered will come out in a few minutes. You are so confident in your expectation that what you ordered is on its way that you create a place for it to land, your place setting, and you frame it with your utensils. Then what do you do... nothing. You sit back enjoy the company of your dining companions with absolute certainty your order will arrive shortly.

Why is this?

Chances are you don't know the waiter personally, so why do you trust them? You don't have any idea who is behind the door that supposedly leads to a kitchen of well-trained cooks with all the ingredients to create your desired meal.

You haven't been back there. You haven't seen the pantry and met the staff and checked their training to make sure they are qualified to cook your meal. Yet all this time you sit there relaxed and totally trusting your meal will be out shortly and it will be served to your liking.

If it was breakfast you ordered perhaps you asked for the eggs over easy and the bacon crisp. If you ordered dinner you may have asked for your steak to be cooked medium rare or you salad to be served with the dressing on the side. No matter what you ordered, you have no doubt your meal will arrive just as you requested. You are trusting the system and you've been trusting systems you really don't know much about your entire life. Trust is something you give, not something someone or some business or organization has to earn.

The truth is someone could do everything "right" and you still may not trust them. So do yourself a favor and stop operating from the myth that others must earn your trust. You own your trust and you give it out as you see fit.

Do you trust that the Divine is on your side?

I promise you this system of divine guidance via your YES has been guiding people to full and happy lives since the beginning of time. Now that's experience you can trust.

— 23 —

Alignment Versus Effort

As we talked about earlier, trusting your feelings is a big part of following your YES, and your feelings aren't in your head. They're in your heart.

If you're in your head, you're disconnected from your feelings. You're trying to intellectualize, "Why do I or don't I feel this way?"

As an intelligent person you've likely been validated for your intellect at various stages in your life. Since we tend to do more of the things we get validated for, your default is to use your brain and your intellect to try and figure things out. Take a moment now and reflect on how often you automatically "think about it" when someone asks you how you feel. Do you tend to look for your feelings in your head or your heart?

Our mind is very powerful. We rely on it all day long to tell us what to do and how to do it. What to wear. What to eat. Where to drive. How to get there and so on. But did you know there is another part of us that is just as important to listen to as our mind and our thoughts: our heart and our feelings.

According to research by the HeartMath Institute[52] the electromagnetic field produced by the heart is 60 times greater in strength than the electromagnetic field generated by the brain. Think about that for a minute. Our heart has 60 times greater strength of attraction for the feelings which align with it than your mind can attract what aligns with your thoughts.

Feelings are powerful. They may not always make sense to our mind, but they are indisputable.

I encourage you to go to your heart and feel things out instead of just trying to figure things out in your head. I gave you a great way to get out of your head and into your heart in the Finding Your YES chapter. I invite you to bookmark it so you can refer to it as often as you need to. (It's on page 31)

Here's a little something I learned from Drs. Joy and Roy Martina[53]: Most people don't realize we have three different levels of processing - the brain, the heart, and the gut. The brain is where we rationalize. It is our logical mind, the details and our creativity. The heart is home to our life missions and passions. The gut is where the courage to move forward resides.

The majority of people go from brain to gut and skip the heart. Their head is the captain of the ship focusing on *how* to do things. For people who are very impulsive, it's the gut, that's the captain of their ship. What most of us have forgotten is the heart was designed to be the captain of the ship because it provides the *what* and the *why* which is what's meant to give us direction in our lives.

Let's say you check in with your heart and notice you are feeling sad. That is the *what*. You ask your heart *why* does this need to change? (Notice you don't ask why do I feel this way, that is not essential to making progress.) Perhaps your answer is because you are crabby and no fun to be around when you are sad, and you want to be happy and enjoyable to be around. Once you know what you want you go to your head to explore *how* your logical mind can make it happen. Your answer might be to go do something you love like take a walk in nature, paint, sing, call a friend etc. Now you tap into the courage which resides in your gut to follow through and do this even if there are a bunch of things on your "to do" list waiting for your attention. It's important to be very clear what part of you is captaining your ship, as it will make a big difference in the choices you make in life.

Start by listening to your heart, your YES, then go to your brain to identify how you're going to act on this, and then to your gut to access the courage to follow through. If you follow those three steps, your decisions become a lot wiser.

Follow your heart but take your brain with you.

- Alfred Adler[54]

Our rational mind thinks if we can figure out how to do something or sort out what's going on, then the solution should be easy. This is another trap we get caught in.

More important than easy is that something be aligned with our truth, our soul, our essence. When you are in alignment it feels easy, even if you're having to do a lot to get to your goal. It's important to understand following your YES doesn't mean just doing the things that feel good. It is doing the things that are aligned with your core essence no matter what, and they can actually be things you're not terribly excited about, like having a difficult conversation with someone you love.

Sometimes your YES is to say *no* to someone. You may be concerned this will disappoint them and you don't feel like disappointing them. That doesn't mean this isn't your YES. It could be bringing something up which has the potential to make the other person feel uncomfortable. It can be frustrating, like needing to repeat a request you have made many times before. It can be saddening, like admitting a relationship is not working out and it is time to move on, none of which feels good. So be aware your YES can be challenging and is not always what you want it to be.

You may not feel like following your YES even when it is aligned with your truth. Remember it is always leading you to growth, expansion and something better in the big scheme of things. No matter how much effort and energy you must put into following your YES, because it's aligned with your heart, your truth and your essence, it doesn't feel draining. It's energizing instead of exhausting.

Recall when you had a difficult conversation with a friend or family member about the "elephant in the room" and even though it took a lot of effort to bring yourself to address whatever the issue was, when it was over you felt energized. This is the result of you following through on what aligned with your heart and speaking your truth.

Let's say your YES is to change your lifestyle, diet-wise. That feels aligned. If changing your diet is really your truth, not just what somebody or society has made you think you need to do, then no matter how dramatic the change is, it will feel natural.

Even though it takes lots of work to clear all the "bad" foods out of your pantry, start shopping differently and break your old eating habits. Such things are hard work, but it doesn't feel like it because it's aligned. Words, actions and behaviors that are aligned energize you.

Something taking no effort does not equal easy. Alignment equals easy, even if there is a great deal of effort involved in following a particular YES. You're in the flow, you're grooving. It may look like a lot of work on the outside, but it doesn't feel that way on the inside.

When you're aligned, life just works. You feel that sense of deep happiness because your higher self is being acknowledged.

- Alexi Panos[55]

When I started writing this book I was dating a woman who lives in Florida, I live in Colorado. We were 2000 miles apart. Neither one of us was specifically looking for a long-distance relationship, and there's nothing easy about all the logistics to make it work, but it totally felt aligned.

Then COVID hit. There was more effort involved in traveling to see each other. Since with every trip we potentially increased our exposure, we agreed to make our visits longer. They were usually a month or more at a time. Now we had to figure out how to work remotely and all those logistics involved even more effort, but even with the extra effort required, it felt easy. I never felt like "OMG, this is so much work!"

Some might say, why don't you just date someone who lives near you. That may be an option, but it may not be aligned and then it would not be easier it would just be more convenient.

This distinction is really key. When we're in alignment, it feels easy and natural, no matter how much activity or effort goes into it.

Understand following your YES may not feel easy right away, because you're unfamiliar with it. Even if it feels wobbly at first, stay with it. The wobbly part is simply that you haven't followed your YES in this way before so it can feel uncertain at first.

Stick with it and keep noting how your YES, your feelings, are guiding you to your highest good and soon the wobble will be gone.

INSIDER TIP

In your past when you were doing what other people or society said you should and disregarding your YES, some people liked you, and some people didn't. This equation doesn't change when you start following your YES.

The difference is now the people who like you and what you're up to actually like the real you instead of some watered-down, compromised version of you that you were being to try to make everybody else happy.

The truth is, you can't please everybody no matter what you do, so you may as well live your truth and be loved by the people who respect and honor you for doing so.

Do what you feel in your heart to be right – for you'll be criticized anyway.

– Eleanor Roosevelt[56]

Your power does not come from effort. Your power comes from alignment. When you are living your life in alignment with your highest good and being your best self is when you are the most powerful. This is the power to give, to receive, to contribute and to love.

— 24 —

Commitment and Your YES

Most of my life I didn't commit to me, the real me. For the most part I just cruised along, not pushing myself and doing just enough to be comfortable. I remember, when I was in high school, seeing a t-shirt in a store which read "I'm #3! I don't try at all" and thinking it was the perfect shirt for me. I even considered buying it, but chose not to *commit* to making that purchase and wearing this message around publicly.

I was afraid the real me wouldn't be enough or perhaps it'd be too much. What if I failed? I spent a lot of time and energy building my risk-avoiding muscles instead of my risk-embracing ones. I accepted *just enough to survive*, but I never realized what I was doing. Truth is, I settled rather than commit to my true self.

I would commit enough to leave the things which *didn't* work for me like jobs or relationships. But I didn't commit to the things that *did* work for me with ease; the things that aligned with my truth, and would support me in thriving instead of just surviving. My YESES.

When I was about 13-years-old I wrote this poem. For a long time I thought it was the definition of who I was. What I didn't realize was it voiced the commitment I'd made subconsciously to struggle. Can you spot the line I'm referring to?

Walking down the middle of the street
Standing in the rain
They both are kind of crazy things to do
But I do them just the same.

They make me feel kind of special
They make me different and that feels good
They make me feel a little bit unreal
If I could do them all the time I would.

I'd rather work my ass off to earn my gold
Than to win it in some game
I know that may sound stupid
But that's just the way I am.

I'm not sure what I'm lookin' for in life
But when I find it, I'll know it's for me
It makes life kind of difficult sometimes
But it also makes me me.

It doesn't matter who wrote this thing at all
It doesn't matter what's my name
What matters is that someday someone might read this
And they might feel the same.

Wouldn't you know, I received many compliments on this poem. Which reinforced that my subconscious, limiting commitment to struggle was a good one: "I'd rather work my ass off to earn my gold."

On some level I was afraid I would not be successful at following my YES and thriving, but I knew how to successfully struggle and survive so I stayed there instead. For decades.

I was like the rosebush that never blooms but doesn't die either. I wasn't bringing my gifts to the world, but at least I was still there.

A rose can grow in virtually every climate on earth, but they don't bloom in every climate.

A bloom on a rose is the gift of the rose. It's not the thorny green plant we see when it's not blooming. When the rose is in bloom is when we get to experience its gifts.

People are the same way. We may be able to live and survive in virtually every environment, but for us to thrive and to blossom we must surround ourselves with the proper environment that supports us in blooming.

This is where following your YES comes in.

Your YES comes from your heart and the commitment you must make to follow it comes from there too. It's emotional not intellectual. When you consistently follow your heart it becomes easier and more natural until it's second nature. Soon it becomes your default. Your commitment to following your YES is exhibited by what you do with your life, and in what you receive back from life.

Think of it this way — what if following your YES was the greatest gift you could ever give anyone? Would you have any resistance to committing to following it then?

If following your YES feels scary or even unnecessary, do it for the people you care about. Do it so you can be your best with them and share your talents with the world.

YES Mastery

I want to share with you a few things that will take your following your YES experience to the next level. The formula you just learned is more than enough to upgrade your life dramatically, but if you want to optimize your practice so you get the most out of your efforts these next few items will take you to an elevated level of life enjoyment.

If you want to master following your YES,
you need to respect it.

— 25 —

Respect Your YES

You must treat your YES with the same reverence you would something you consider to be sacred, because indeed it is sacred. After all, your YES comes to you from the Divine.

Sometimes you may feel like you need to justify or explain or defend your YES, but it doesn't need defending. To justify means to show or prove to be right or reasonable. We want to justify when we are worried people won't understand, or we feel our YES might be judged by others as selfish or unreasonable. I promise you, your YES *will* be misunderstood by some, this is inevitable. Christopher Columbus had a YES. He was determined to find a direct water route west from Europe to Asia. He believed he could sail west across the Atlantic Ocean, instead of around Africa, and reach Asia. In doing so he could bring back rich cargoes of silks and spices more quickly. For over a decade he petitioned the monarchs of England, France, and Portugal to support his expedition. They all told him his YES was unreasonable, but he respected his YES as something sacred and eventually gained the support of King Ferdinand II and Queen Isabella I of Spain. By continuing to honor and respect his YES he found the people who were in alignment with his calling. Christopher Columbus never discovered a shorter route to Asia, but he did stumble upon something virtually no one in Europe was aware of at that time - the Americas.

Understand that the right to choose your own path is a sacred privilege. Use it. Dwell in possibility.

- Oprah Winfrey[57]

Often you can't justify your YES even if you want to, because you can't possibly comprehend how what's being presented to you in the moment will contribute to your path in the future.

Remember how I followed my YES to move to Colorado and within hours of arriving I had a great place to live without ever looking in the paper or talking to a real estate agent? What I didn't tell you was I moved to Colorado just 30 days after returning from my vacation. You may recall the phone call I had with my friend Shelly which led to me sub-letting my place and selling her all the furniture I was not taking with me just 15 minutes after I arrived home from my trip. My next call was to my younger brother Steve. When he picked up the phone I said, "Guess what?" He immediately replied with absolute certainty, "You're moving to Colorado." I about fell over since other than Shelly no one knew I was even considering moving.

I asked, "What made you say that?"

He replied, "When we visited Aunt Betty and Uncle Bob in Colorado when we were in grade school the entire trip you kept saying, 'I'm gonna live here. I'm gonna live here.' over and over. It drove me and Tim (our older brother) crazy because you wouldn't stop saying it." (I didn't remember doing this at all.)

Steve said as soon as I told him I was going to Colorado for vacation he knew I would move there. And he was right. Eighteen years after I had my first YES about living in Colorado I was finally moving there.

The thing was I still didn't know why I was so drawn to Colorado or what I would find when I got there so there was no way I could justify or explain or defend the move I was making.

Many of my friends and family were shocked. It all seemed so sudden to them. They had no idea this had been incubating for 18 years. I didn't really have a plan. I had a calling.

My YES in the moment was to move to Boulder, Colorado. Where I would live or what I would do for a living etc. honestly didn't even enter my mind. When I think back, I realize I hadn't even considered those things. I was following this one YES in present time knowing it would lead to another when the time was right.

The next YES, as you know, was walking downtown in Boulder, meeting Marcia, going to dinner with her friends, and a place to live was mine by the end of the night. My next YES showed up the following day. I was unpacking my car and moving things into my new home when I realized other than Marcia and the people I had met at dinner the night before, I really didn't know anyone in Boulder. I wanted to change this. My YES was quite simple. I needed to find a way to meet people.

I grabbed a local newspaper looking for events or activities where I might meet like-minded people. I found a presentation happening that night that sounded good and decided to attend. I don't remember what the topic of the event was, but when I got there, I knew I had chosen well because the room was packed.

It was so packed that every seat was taken and we were standing 2 and 3 people deep in the aisle and all across the back of the room. I was amazed at how large and enthusiastic the crowd was. The speaker was great and when the event was over, we literally had to unpack the room in the same order we had entered it, one by one. As I was standing there awaiting my turn to leave I saw a guy walking down the aisle towards the back of the room who I knew. It was Greg who was also a guest at the house I had stayed at during my vacation in Boulder one month earlier. I was surprised to see him since his plan when we last spoke was to leave Boulder a couple of days after I did. Just then he saw me and signaled he'd wait for me outside. I don't know why I did this, but once I got outside, even before I said hello I asked him, "Do you still go to those healing thingies?"

See, the last night of my vacation Greg and I had plans to take our hosts to dinner on Pearl Street. When we met at 6:00 I was informed Greg was going to some healing thing and would join us shortly. We decided to have a beer and wait for him. Six o'clock turned to 6:30 and then 7. This was pre cell phone days so we had no way of finding out what was keeping him so we had a couple of rounds of beers and shared some nachos while we waited for Greg to arrive. By 7:30 we were all pretty hungry and a little frustrated with Greg, so we went ahead and ordered dinner. Just before 8:00 Greg came walking up Pearl Street beaming. He had a huge smile on his face and couldn't have looked happier. He apologized profusely and told us the "healing thing" he went to was only 15 minutes but afterward they had an opening for a psychic reading and offered it to him which is why he was so late. The rest of us had no idea what Greg was talking about. None of us knew what a healing was, and certainly did not know what a psychic reading was. But Greg couldn't stop talking about it. The two guys we had been staying with weren't interested at all and just wanted to flirt with the girls walking by our street-side table. I didn't have a clue what Greg was talking about either, but something about it interested me so I listened as he went on and on about energy and what they told him about his chakras and his aura.

This is the "healing thingie" I was referring to as we stood there in the hall a month later. I think he was as shocked as I was at my question, but he replied, "Yeah, I do. But if you want me to take you we have to go tomorrow night because I am moving to Aspen on Thursday." And that's just what we did. The following night I met Greg outside of the Psychic Horizons Center (PHC) on Arapahoe Avenue in Boulder, Colorado. I was about to go to my first healing clinic even though I still did not know what one really was or what I was getting myself into.

Funny thing was it ended up being not all that interesting to me. I didn't really understand what they did and there was no big "Ah-ha" moment. It was fine, but I was not sure I would do it again, and I couldn't understand why Greg got so excited about getting healings. We went to dinner afterwards and Greg told me stories of other energy work he had received all around the world. Again, it was interesting, but I didn't feel called to explore it further. Shortly after this all the YESES I had been following since I decided to move to Colorado started to make sense to me.

The next day Greg moved to Aspen and the following week I found myself at my local grocery store right down the street from PHC at the time the healing clinic was happening. My YES was to go get another healing, so I did.

This happened the next couple of weeks as well. The fourth time I went in for a healing one of the teachers there, Teresa, gave me the healing and afterwards said, "I noticed you have been here several times. Would you be interested in learning how to give these healings yourself? We have a class starting next week where you will learn how to give healings."

My response was, "What is this place?" I really didn't know. I just showed up once a week, walked in, got a healing, ten minutes later I left a donation and walked out, but I never really looked around.

Teresa laughed and gave me a little tour explaining as we went that they taught people how to follow their internal guidance, read energy and work with the chakras and aura.

I had no idea what any of this stuff was and really hadn't felt like I got much out of the healings, but, and I swear this is exactly what I thought, "It sounds more interesting than what's on TV, so why not?" And I signed up for class. No justification needed other than it was my YES in the moment.

Little did I know the class I had just signed up for would be the first step in me developing my skills as an energy reader, becoming a teacher, a minister and staff member of the center. Ultimately it has led me to teaching classes and workshops around the world with students from every corner of the planet.

There was no way I could have justified following my YES and moving to Colorado a few weeks earlier as I packed up my things back in Illinois, because I had no idea what was waiting for me when I got there. This will happen to you too. Don't worry about justifying your YES, just own it and respect it.

Trust the divine guidance that is your YES.

Your YES is yours, and you don't need to justify it to anyone.

While you don't need to justify your YES, you may have to protect it, because sometimes you're the only one who gets it. Your YES is yours. Not anyone else's. So the people around you may very well try and talk you out of it. Not because they don't want you to have your YES and be happy and fulfilled, but because they don't understand it. They feel it's their responsibility to "protect" you from what may appear to them to be a crazy, irrational or risky idea, and therefore "protecting" you is the best thing they can do as a friend, family member, or colleague.

We've all had times in our life when our next step feels so clear to us and yet the people around us all question it and try to persuade us to do something else. It could be regarding starting or ending a relationship, taking a particular job, or making a major investment financially like a purchasing a home or buying into a business venture. At the same time you could feel pressured about your clothing selections, who you spend time with or what you choose to eat. As well intended as their suggestions may be, it can still feel like you're all alone in your YES.

You may have been taught to value the guidance and opinions of others more than you do your own guidance and opinions. Taught you should only follow your guidance if it is validated by someone else. We talked about this in the Inner Authority chapter. What someone else is offering may come from the best of intentions, but it's up to you to protect your YES and say "Thanks, but no thanks. I appreciate your input, but I am still taking this next step because it feels aligned with my truth."

> The most compassionate people have the most well defined and well respected boundaries. They assume that other people are doing the best they can, but they also ask for what they need and they don't put up with a lot of crap.[58]
>
> - Brene Brown - *Rising Strong*

Transformational and dating coach Marni Battista[59] provides a great illustration of one way we can give our authority over to someone else and by doing so we abandon our YES instead of protecting it.

Marni was working with a business coach, but something wasn't lining up. She actually had sent a series of emails to this coach saying "I don't think this is a good idea." And the business coach replied, "This is just your fear talking." As someone who tries to be super coachable Marni is always looking for her limits, and the coach was saying, "Oh, it's just a limit." So she bought into that intellectually and dismissed what her heart was telling her.

She knew the advice and suggestions she was receiving were never going to work for her and her company, but all her rationalizing of "I hired them" and "I want to be a good student" and "Maybe it is just my fear" led her to not follow through and honor her YES. Marni chose to respect her business coach's suggestions more than she respected her YES. She didn't listen to her YES, and it was a major disaster.

Whenever you are tempted to do like Marni and put the input of another above your own ask yourself this question: Who is inherently equipped to know what is best for you, someone else or you?

If you are a person who has a history of disrespecting your YES it may be challenging in the beginning for you to respect your YES more than you do others' opinions or suggestions, so you will need to build up this muscle of saying "Thanks, but no thanks." Know that through commitment and consistency in following your YES this muscle will strengthen quickly.

Your YES deserves your respect. If you don't respect it no one else will either.

— 26 —

Preemptive Healing

Preemptive healing is this sneaky little thing we do with all the best intentions, which ends up keeping everyone involved from being their best, and it happens when we justify to ourselves why we *shouldn't* follow our YES.

We do this when we think our partner, our friend, our parents, our co-workers etc. won't be able to survive the consequences of us following our YES. So we don't do what's right for ourselves because we think they can't handle it. Nobody wins. Here's how this played out for a client of mine.

Julie had long blond hair that she had worn the same way since she was a little girl. Her mother used to brush it for her every morning before she went to school, and was always so proud when someone would comment on how beautiful her daughter's hair was.

At the time I worked with Julie she was in her mid-40s and told me she had wanted to cut her hair ever since she moved out of her parent's home when she was 18, but she was afraid to cut it because she was convinced it meant so much to her mom and cutting it would break her mother's heart.

Julie was sure her mother would be devastated if she cut her hair. So instead of living her life in the way that made her happiest and being her best, she kept her hair long and straight. Julie invested tons of time washing, drying and brushing it out every day for no other reason than she did not think her mother could handle it if she were to change her hair style.

Finally, Julie decided she had the strength she needed to cut it. She was scared but she did it. Her stylist was thrilled. She had been encouraging Julie to try something new for years.

As her hair was being cut, she could feel the weight of years of holding herself back being released.

When the styling was complete Julie looked in the mirror with a huge smile on her face and absolutely loved her new look. A moment later the smile disappeared as she thought of her mother. How would she ever tell her mother what she had done? For weeks Julie avoided her parents. Making up reasons for not coming over for dinner and avoiding getting together with them for fear of how her mother would react. Finally the day came when Julie could not avoid her mother any longer. It was her mother's birthday and she had to attend the family birthday dinner. As Julie walked to the door of the home she grew up in she had never been more nervous. She was so nervous she actually knocked on the door instead of walking in. Her mother answered and as soon as she opened the door she exclaimed "You cut your hair!" then just stared. Julie dreaded her worst fear was being realized. She just knew she had broken her mother's heart.

After what seemed like an eternity her mother said, "I'm so happy you did this. I love it! I always wondered how you would choose to wear your hair."

Julie couldn't believe it. Her mother was happy she cut her hair.

For over 20 years she had worn her hair long and straight for fear her mother would be devastated and instead she was excited.

This is a great example of how we hold ourselves back from fully expressing ourselves because we fear someone else could not handle the changes we need to make to live our truth. We think we are saving someone. In truth, preemptive healing is disrespecting them and their journey. Who are we to decide if someone else can handle us changing and growing? When we preemptively heal, we steal that opportunity for growth from them and sell ourselves short at the same time.

You following your YES might turn out to be a growth opportunity for them. Your YES could inspire them. It could be exactly what they need to experience to step into their YES.

Preemptive healing can also be a way of hiding and living a deferred life. We tell ourselves we are not living our truth because someone else couldn't handle it, but often it's simply an excuse for staying closed off from our truth. We convince ourselves we're being kind, generous, considerate or sensitive to the other person. In reality we're invalidating them by acting like they can't handle the life they've created as we avoid what we know to be true for ourselves..

While writing this book, I met with my friend Millie for dinner to talk about her feedback on an early draft she had generously reviewed for me. She mentioned how reading the manuscript helped her recognize a "big fat ball of tension" in her life. Opportunities to spend time with family, travel to a friend's surprise 50th birthday party in Florida and several other upcoming events were conflicting with a training week she was scheduled to attend at the same time. The training no longer felt like her YES as it had when she started two years earlier. A great deal had happened over those two years, and because of that and the work of the program itself, she felt her priorities had changed.

I encouraged her to feel into her heart and see what would be most supportive of her being her best right now. She laughed at how clear her answer was and said, "I need to drop out of the program." And then let out a big sigh of relief.

A couple of days later I received this text from her:

> *Well, just sent my official "I'm not going to ___ Training" email and I'm sitting here bawling my eyes out. I know it's because I'm relieved and proud of myself for doing what is right by me!*

My reply was: *Bravo! feel the freedom of owning your YES!*

Millie later told me that minutes after sending her resignation, the founder of the program called her to say "I'm proud of you," and admitted she was personally sad because she loved having her in the program and wondered when they would see each other next, but she could tell this was the right next step for her.

This is what's available to you when you stop buying into stories that you are doing others a favor by not following your YES.

Your YES comes from the Divine, and I promise you, just as all the plants and animals and nature works in a symbiotic fashion, so do our YESES. The Divine has created this so your YES, my YES and everyone else's all work well together. It doesn't mean we'll always like the responses we get in the moment. We may be frustrated by somebody's response. We may wonder why can't they be more supportive? Managing how someone responds to your YES is not your job.

Your job, your one and only job, is to share your one-of-a-kind expression of the Divine with the world.

If we take good care of ourselves, we help everyone.

- Thích Nhat Hanh[60]

There's nothing selfish about following your YES. The most generous thing you can possibly do is bring the most complete version of you to every person, every situation, every experience you have each day.

— 27 —

Obvious Is Not Obvious

A potential pitfall of following your YES is that you may start to think your YESES are obvious to everyone since they are now so obvious to you. Ninety-nine times out of a hundred this is not the case.

When your YES feels obvious to you, always clarify. Don't take for granted it is as clear for everyone else as it is for you and then get frustrated when others don't act or respond in the way you expected.

I'm not talking about being Captain Obvious and declaring things like: the sky is blue, water is wet or when a package of nuts has a warning on it stating that this product may contain nuts. That is not what we are talking about here.

There are two potential outcomes from stating what seems obvious when it comes to your YES, and they are both positive. Usually it reveals what you thought was obvious was not clear to the other party. When this is the case you can now clarify and set both of you up to win.

Occasionally stating what you think is obvious will confirm that indeed it was clear to them as well. No harm done. Now you know for certain you are on the same page which provides peace of mind for everyone.

So you win either way, but our nature is to suppose: "That's so obvious I don't have to express it. Everybody knows that." No they don't! You'll be surprised how many times the other person will respond something like: "What? I had no idea. I'm glad you told me, now it makes perfect sense."

For some reason we tend to assume when we learn things that feel obvious to us that we must be the last one to know, and expressing it would be a waste of everyone's time. It isn't!

At one point in my dating life I was seeing a woman named Susan. I was falling in love with her, but I didn't think she felt the same way about me. Her words and actions led me to believe that she was just interested in having fun but nothing more. I thought it was obvious how I felt, and since I was convinced she did not feel the same way I said to her, "I don't feel the way you do about our relationship, so I think we should part ways." She said, "If that's how you feel, then I guess we're done," and she left.

Several weeks later I saw Susan at an event our mutual friends were hosting and at one point in the evening we found ourselves alone. She said to me, "I cried every day for a month after we broke up. I was so in love with you." I was dumbstruck. When I said to her, "I don't feel the way you do ..." what she heard was "I don't love you." The truth was I did love her and I thought she didn't love me. Turns out I was wrong in my assumption that how she felt was obvious to me. And in thinking how I felt was obvious to her I was wrong again. I asked why she hadn't called or reached out in any way and she said I was so clear I didn't feel like she did that she thought reaching out would just lead to more pain.

Obvious is not obvious was a brutal lesson to learn.

Next time you think to yourself "Oh this YES is so obvious." Do yourself and everyone else a favor by clarifying to make sure it is as obvious to them as it is to you. You have nothing to lose and everything to gain.

— 28 —

Weird is Normal

In many ways "being yourself" in our culture has been deemed a bad thing. Conformity is what gets rewarded. The last thing you want to be is weird or an outsider, that's unacceptable. You're supposed to be "normal."

Normality is a paved road: It's comfortable to walk, but no flowers grow.

- Vincent van Gogh[61]

According to a review published by two Yale psychologists in *Trends in Cognitive Sciences* we are all a little bit weird. Being weird is, in fact, totally normal. Senior author Avram J. Holmes, Ph.D., summed up the findings by stating, "I would argue that there is no fixed normal." "Any behavior is neither solely negative or solely positive. There are potential benefits for both, depending on the context you're placed in."[62]

We use the word weird a lot and yet I bet the original meaning of the word weird will surprise you. According to the *New Oxford American Dictionary*, weird originally meant 'having the power to control destiny.' WOW! That's not at all how we use this word in modern society is it?

Where once being weird was a good thing, eventually the powers that were realized if everyone was being weird they could not be controlled. How can you control a group where everyone is controlling their own destiny?

How brilliant. If you want to control a group of people, you certainly don't want them to control their own destiny so you make the word that means just that into something undesirable. Then, because labels are so powerful and most people don't want to be labeled as weird, people voluntarily give up control of their own destiny. They give up their YES.

I don't know about you, but this true definition doesn't sound so bad to me. In fact now when someone says something I do, wear, or a perspective I have is "weird", I reply "Thank you!" I usually get a strange look because they don't know the true meaning of weird, but I do. And now you do too.

We are all a little weird
and life's a little weird,
and when we find someone
whose weirdness is compatible with ours,
we join up with them and fall in mutual weirdness
and call it love.[63]

- Robert Fulghum

Following your YES can be viewed as weird by others and they're right. When you follow your YES you're enthusiastically adopting the power to control destiny — your destiny. So should someone call your YES weird, simply reply "Thank You" and let them wonder. After all, sticks and stones ... .

Flucky

I have referenced flow and being in your flow several times in this book and I want to make sure I am clear about what I mean by flow. After all, what's obvious to me may not be obvious to you. :-)

Flow is a mindset. A way of engaging in life from a place of curiosity and exuberance. When you are in the flow you are in a state of peak experiences, which foster productivity, success, and fulfillment. This state has been given the name "flow" because people often made the analogy of moving effortlessly in a current of energy where action and awareness follow each other spontaneously and freely as being "carried by a river or a stream."

According to Mihály Csíkszentmihályi[64] the Hungarian-American psychologist who recognized and named the psychological concept of flow - "Flow is a mental state in which a person performing an activity is fully immersed in a feeling of energized focus, full involvement, and enjoyment."

Another common phrase for flow is "being in the zone." Being in the zone is commonly associated with things like sports, dancing, painting, and yoga, but you can be in the zone or in the flow with pretty much anything like cooking, chopping wood, or writing a book. I was in the flow myself when I wrote the first draft of this book in six days. Everything just seemed to effortlessly come together.

People ask me how I make music. I tell them I just step into it.
It's like stepping into a river and joining the flow.
Every moment in the river has its song.

- Michael Jackson[65]

While having coffee and discussing this book with one of my favorite people in the world, my friend Anna came up with a fantastic term — flucky, which means flowing with luck. This is the state of flow that you can experience when you trust your YES consistently. Everything I have shared with you in this book is designed to help you be flucky. Allow me to provide an example of what fluckiness can look like.

— 29 —

Free Beer

Our story of Fluck begins when three guys stepped into the water at Eben G. Fine Park to go tubing down Boulder Creek. Two of them decided to just kick back, relax, and trust the flow of the creek to carry them to their destination. The other guy kept trying to steer and control where he went. He didn't trust the flow of the creek. He was afraid it was going to crash him into rocks. He was splashing around, fighting the current and having a wretched time.

That day I happened to be sitting on the shore reading a book when they floated past me. The first two guys who were relaxed and trusting the flow waved and said, "This is awesome. It's so much fun!" But when the other guy, who was fighting the flow went by, he looked over at me and said, "This is miserable. It's the dumbest thing I've ever done."

Now on this day, something very interesting happened. As these three men were floating down the stream, cans of beer started appearing in the creek. Apparently someone had placed a case of beer in the creek upstream to keep it cool and the box had opened up in the water and their beers were escaping.

As the beers started floating past me I looked downstream and noticed the first two guys spot the beers and paddle over to grab them. They exclaimed, "How awesome is this, the creek even gives you free beer!"

The only time the guys who were trusting the flow paddled to change their direction was to receive more gifts and support from the creek.

Meanwhile, the man who was fighting the flow was too busy to even notice the free beer floating by him. He was still convinced that if he did not direct every moment of his journey down the creek he would be dashed upon the rocks and be drowned. The other thing he didn't realize is the creek was only a foot and a half deep, so even if he got dumped out of his tube, all he had to do was stand up and he'd be fine.

The flow is always flowing. It flows at different rates of speed at different times. Sometimes it goes over rapids, sometimes it gets splashed up on rocks and then rolls back into the stream and sometimes it gets hung up in eddies for a while, but eventually it always reaches its destination much like the water in the creek would ultimately reach the ocean.

Trust the flow. Relax and keep your eyes open for the bonus gifts it has for you that you never would have expected, like the free beers floating in the creek.

Every drop of water takes its own path to the ocean. No two are the same, but they all get there and you will reach your divinely intended destination too, when you trust the flow, YOUR flow.

The continual series of YESES in your life is the flow. Follow it. Trust it. Moment to moment and your life will be filled with ease and grace ... and who knows perhaps some free beer too.

A can of beer floating in the creek is not a very big item to see, but to someone who is tuned to the abundance of YESES in their life, it stands out like a neon light in the dark.

When we are in the vibration of flow and abundance good things keep coming to us.

Chances are you have a colleague or friend or family member who seems to always have things easy. Everything seems to work out for them. And just when it looks like everything's going perfectly for them, something even better shows up in their world. This is The Universe showing you what's available when you tune into the abundance of YESES in life that make up the flow.

Take a minute right now and reflect on a time in your life where things just seemed to line up or you experienced a happy accident. Where you did something out of the norm and it led to something wonderful.

Perhaps you went to an event or a store or travelled a different route that you never go and you weren't really sure why you were doing it, and then you ran into a dear friend you hadn't seen for years or found an item you couldn't find anywhere else or it was on sale for a killer price.

We often dismiss these kind of experiences as simply being serendipities or luck or destiny. When you follow your YES these kind of events become the norm in your life.

I've never really done anything to create what has happened. It creates itself. I'm here because it happened. But I didn't do anything to make it happen apart from saying "Yes."

- Ringo Starr[66]

Every one of the "happy accidents" you've experienced occurred because you followed your internal guidance that may or may not have made any sense to you in the moment, but you followed it anyway and it led you to something wonderful and unexpected.

Just this week I received a call from my friend Cam and as we were talking about his vision of starting a mushroom farm my friends Amy and Brian, the couple whose straw bale house I helped build in New York, popped into my mind. I couldn't imagine why they came into my awareness. They have a small farm, but it wasn't really what Cam was talking about.

I decided to trust this YES and introduce Cam to them.

A couple days later Cam calls me back and says, "You won't believe this! Amy said they are looking for a partner for the horse sanctuary they run."

As it turned out, another part of Cam's vision was creating a horse sanctuary and healing center where people can come to get healed by interacting with horses. I didn't even know Amy and Brian had this horse sanctuary, and yet my YES to introduce them aligned with Cam's YES to start a sanctuary and Amy and Brian's YES to find a partner.

You'll find when someone says to you "you won't believe this," like Cam did, it will make you smile because you now know as someone who follows their YES that the Divine is coordinating things and there is no limit to what's available. When you're following your YES you believe everything is possible because part of the process is staying open to possibilities.

Remember what Yoda said: The reason we fail is because we don't believe.

Most people would think what transpired between Cam, Amy, Brian and I was lucky, but the truth is it was divine guidance and this guidance is always flowing and available to us whenever we choose to pay attention to it. Following your YES is the shortcut to fluckiness.

— 30 —

Control Versus Flow

Many people, like the guy who was splashing around in his inner tube, are terrified to let go of control and trust the flow. They believe if they're in control, then they can limit any potential damage. If this doesn't go where they think it's meant to go, then they've already managed the outcome. They've controlled their exposure, and therefore what they've risked.

The belief is, if we control everything, then we're not risking anything.

One of my favorite jokes is:

How do you make God laugh?

I don't know ...

Tell 'em your plans.

I told this joke to a friend of mine and she said, "God must laugh a lot!"

What I love about this joke is it is such a great reminder that our ideas of how to control situations are irrelevant. There is a divine plan at work and the sooner we stop trying to control it the more ease and enjoyment we'll experience.

One of the things that *feels* like control to us is confidence about an outcome. This is easier to feel about things we have experience with, but where we get tripped up is when we need to do things that are new to us. Confidence is about the known. I'm confident this restaurant has good food. Why? Because I've eaten here before. The first time you go to a restaurant, you don't have any confidence they have good food, but you're courageous enough to give it a shot. You can go to that restaurant and it's terrible, but unless you had the courage to walk in the door and give it a shot, you'll never know for sure.

It's the same thing with relationships: You need to have the courage to think. "It's true I haven't experienced a loving partnership yet, but that's not going to stop me from being courageous enough to own what I really want and give it a shot."

Sometimes when you are following your YES the guidance you receive will be to pursue something familiar and confidence will be available to you. There will also be YESES guiding you to do or say or experience something that is new. This is when you must substitute waiting to have confidence before you take action with the courage to give it a chance. Open to the possibility that following this YES could be as good or even better than what you have experienced before.

One of my clients, Jessica, came up with this great term: **Funcertainty**.

> She said, "Funcertainty is what happens when you let go of control, don't give a shit, and trust the Universe."

This is perfect. When you let go of control and trust the Universe to have your back, you turn uncertainty into **funcertainty**.

Epilogue

— 31 —

"What If I Can't Do This?"

You may be thinking following your YES sounds difficult. You may feel like you are so far away from where you want to be that there is no way you can possibly reach your dreams and your goals. You may be wondering if you are too immersed in your NOs and your Maybes to start following your YES at this stage in your life. I get it, and you are not the only person with this concern.

Stepping onto a brand-new path is difficult, but not more difficult than remaining in a situation, which is not nurturing to the whole woman/man.

- Maya Angelou[67]

Unfortunately, our culture has become so addicted to immediate, extraordinary results that if we don't experience an instant major victory, we deem ourselves a failure. We have come to expect that making changes in our lives will be like turning on the lights. Just flip the switch and immediately our world goes from dark to light.

We often hear people say when they had an "Ah-ha" moment or a revelation, that "it was like a light went on." I want you to understand that following your YES is waaaay simpler than what it takes for a light to turn on. Here's a little something I learned a few years ago about turning on a light that most people don't know.

I was attending a presentation by an inventor who was developing technology to streamline the integration of solar energy into the power grid, and he explained when you flip a light switch to turn on the lights between 45 to 50 different interactions have to take place in precise sequence for your lights to come on. Everything including the electricity generation source at the power plant, all the different transformers, the transmission lines, the substations, the wiring and junctions in your house all the way to the light switch, they all have to work in perfect synchrony in order for the light to come on when you flick the switch.

Yet we never doubt something this complex will work every time. It is our expectation that when we flip the switch, the light comes on. So, what does this have to do with following your YES?

Following your YES only requires two actions to happen for the result we desire, for our light to come on — not 45 or 50 actions — two. It's a much simpler process.

What are the two things, you ask?

The first one is, you guessed it: **Follow your YES.** This is you deciding to pay attention to your feelings, listen to your divine guidance, which is always given to us in feelings, and consciously choose to act. What you're doing, your action, is a choice not a wish. The action you must take is to consciously engage in actively choosing to pay attention to your guidance and follow your YES, even if you have no idea why this is what you're getting as guidance or where it is taking you. You can do that can't you?

So, what's the second thing? **The Divine has to be supporting you.** The Divine must be sending you guidance and energy. If we use our analogy of the light switch, the Divine is the power source sending this power to you in the form of your YES, and your job is to be the light switch that makes the connection and receives the energy completing the circuit. When you do this your light will go on instantly, every time.

Here's the deal.

Without question, I can 100% guarantee you the Divine is always doing its part. Always. It never stops being in alignment with you and why can I say this with such certainty? Because you are the Divine and the Divine is you. You are an extension of the Divine. So how could it possibly stop being there for you? You are it and it is you.

There you have it. For you to be successful at following your YES two things have to happen, and one is guaranteed. How much simpler can this get?

The only variable is you, and you have total control over you.

Just know when you're worrying about, "I don't know if I can do this" it's because you're imagining this is some complex system with many components that are outside of your control.

Following your YES is very, very, simple.

Being afraid to follow your YES is normal.

Do it anyway!

I invite you to give yourself permission to expect following your YES to work perfectly. When you do you will no longer need to doubt, worry or fret.

— 32 —

"Can't" Never Did Anything

When I was growing up, anytime I told my Dad I couldn't do something, he would reply, "Can't never did anything." As annoying as that was to hear, I knew he was right. Think about it. Name one thing that has ever been attributed to can't. The Wright brothers had a bicycle shop. They were not aeronautical engineers. Why were they the first ones who succeeded in developing motorized flight? It certainly was not because they told themselves they can't. When they interview Tom Brady after he has won yet another Super Bowl, (he's won seven so far), the reporter always asks what he attributes the success of his team to. Not once has he, or any other athlete for that matter, ever said, "I want to thank 'can't'. Without 'can't' we wouldn't have won this title." No one has ever said this because "Can't never did anything." It's said that Thomas Edison failed over 1,000 times before he discovered the proper combination of materials to create the incandescent light bulb. He had over 1,000 opportunities to say "I can't" but he didn't because ... say it with me, "Can't never did anything."

I shared with you earlier that I used to host a radio show. On the day I launched my talk radio show my primary area of expertise that qualified me for hosting a show was I could talk. I did have one other area of expertise which was in the use of *can't* to create long lists of objections to stop me from even considering starting a radio show in the first place. Things like - I can't launch a radio show because:

- I have never done this before
- I know nothing about broadcasting
- I know nothing about promoting a show
- I don't have any guests
- No one knows who I am
- No one is going to tune into someone they don't know
- And many, many more

In the past I'd had a tendency to let can't win, and these objections invariably would have convinced me to bail out on this dream. This time my dream won.

Nothing will ever be attempted if all possible objections must be first overcome.

- Jules Lederer[68]

Because I didn't let *can't* stop me, that show ended up impacting the lives of thousands of listeners in over 100 countries every week. All of this happened without me ever learning how to produce or broadcast a show or coming to understand the technology behind the show any more than I did when I started. Those things weren't my YES. Hosting the show was. Throughout my life, whenever I would get frustrated and think I was crazy for pursuing a dream I heard my father's voice saying "can't never did anything." It reminded me I can either argue for my limitations or fight for my dreams. I like the dreams better.

So, what is your idea? Not the safe idea you know you can accomplish, but the one that scares you and eats at you. There is no wrong answer, just own it for yourself.

Next time you hear yourself saying "I can't" refocus on what you *can* do. And should your YES involve things you don't have the training or skills to do, know there are people out there whose YES is to do just those things. When you bring those YESES together, that's when the magic happens.

— 33 —

Experience is the Teacher

I'm a strong believer that words don't teach; life experience does. This may sound kind of strange from a man who just wrote a book, but I'm serious. Let me show you what I mean.

When you were a child people surely told you not to touch a flame, a stove, a BBQ grill or anything else that was hot because it would burn you. Did you do it anyway? Did you still end up touching something really hot, intentionally or unintentionally, at some point before you truly understood what they were saying? I did. I will never forget when I was about 6-years-old and accidentally touched the side of the grill while I was toasting a marshmallow. I jumped back and inadvertently stepped on our cat's tail, who then bit my ankle, causing me to leap forward and burn myself on the grill again, resulting in me dropping my marshmallow on the ground. I'm not sure if it was my burnt arm, the cat bite or the lost marshmallow that hurt the most. I have no idea what words were said to me about avoiding getting burnt, but I can still feel the experience of that lesson as if it were yesterday.

This is exactly why only reading this book will not change your life.

Reading this book did not build any YES following muscles in you yet. You now understand what following your YES is all about, the importance of it, how it benefits you and others, plus you have many examples of what following a YES looks like in the real world, and a formula to follow, but as for actual YES following muscles, you have no more now than when you cracked the cover on this book. Much like if you read a book on fitness, you would not become more fit by reading the book. You must take what you learned in these pages and apply it in your life so you can experience it. This is required if you're going to embody following your YES as your new default operating system.

You could be the kind of person who has aspirations to apply the things you learn, but experience has shown you this is not what actually happens.

You start with the best of intentions and then worry you aren't totally sure how to apply what you've learned. You certainly don't want to make things worse, so perhaps you should just stay where you are. After all, you know you can survive where you are. You've been surviving it for years.

It may surprise you to know only 2% of people who read books like this apply what they've learned on their own long enough for it to result in a permanent transformation. The rest need additional assistance to integrate the information into their daily behaviors in order to enhance their life. If you're ready to stop just surviving and start blooming, then I implore you to get some support. Join a program or community or engage a mentor. Let your YES guide you.

The important part is you get the support you need so you don't waste the momentum you have built up and the time you have invested by reading this book.

Isn't it odd? Of all the people in all the world who are
starting to "get it," how few actually give it to themselves.
I think it's because they forget to live it.
Just knowing the truth is not enough, because just
knowing it, without living it, is the same as not knowing it.[69]

- The Universe

If you like my style and want more of this then go to:

www.followyouryes.com/program

and check out what's available to support you in becoming an expert at living your YES so you can enjoy the ease, joy and flow that it brings.

My greatest desire is that you apply what you have learned here so it can change your life. There is an old saying that knowledge is power, yet sadly this is wrong. Knowledge is not power. If it was then libraries would be the most powerful places on Earth. It is the application of knowledge that is power. Don't just understand how to follow your YES, live it.

— 34 —

How Bad Do You Want It?

As I mentioned at the very beginning of this book, there is an element of risk in following your YES, and one of the things that often feels most risky is making a commitment to apply what we have learned.

Success is not built around convenience. It's built around commitment.

- Marc Von Musser[70]

Commitments are formal promises we make to ourselves, another person, our family, our employer, to friends or mentors etc.

In recent years western culture has become more and more commitment averse. Nowadays it is much more common to hear someone say they will *try* instead of committing. Instead of saying "I will definitely be there" we say "I'll *try* and make it." Instead of making a specific commitment to eat less sugar or fewer carbs we put out a vague intention of "I'll *try* and eat better." Instead of "I'm devoted to having a more fulfilling career" we say "I'm gonna *try* and find a different job." Trying is much more popular than committing.

Let me share a little secret with you ... *try* is a lie.

Think about it, the last time you were invited to a dinner, a party or an event where you said you would *try* and attend, did you make it? I'll bet you didn't. (I didn't either.)

Try is very popular because you can't really fail at *trying*.

How many people do you know who have tried to lose 10 pounds year after year but they never seem to accomplish this goal? Did they fail if they didn't lose the weight? No, because if they made some effort, no matter how small, they succeeded at *trying* even if they didn't reach their goal.

If you genuinely want to elevate your life personally, professionally, romantically or financially you will have to do more than *try*. You must commit. People often tell me they don't like committing because if they don't reach their goal they will feel like a failure. I get that. Nobody likes to fail. So let me share a secret with you that will assure you never fail at something you have committed to ever again.

Are you ready?

> Whenever you don't reach your goal on your first attempt, recommit to it and keep going.

Most people think committing to something is what you do once, and if you don't reach your goal on your first attempt you have failed. The true power in commitment is in recommitting as often as necessary. There is not a single business leader who has ever been on the cover of Forbes magazine who didn't recommit repeatedly before they reached their goal. There is not a single married couple celebrating their 10th, 25th or 50th wedding anniversary who did not have to recommit to each other countless times to reach this milestone.

Recommitting is what we do whenever we get off course. It is the key to succeeding.

Do you know one of the reasons many fitness and weight loss programs build in what are called cheat meals or cheat days? Because it takes the pressure off.

You are actually encouraged to not be perfect and give yourself a break from the pursuit of your goal with the full understanding you'll get right back on the program once your cheat meal or cheat day is over. It is built-in recommitment.

The day after my 40th birthday I started The Steps Across America event which I introduced you to in chapter 12 - Permission to be a Beginner. Myself and eleven other brave/crazy souls were walking from Chelsea Pier in New York City to Santa Monica Pier in California to promote fitness in celebration of the Presidential Council on Fitness's 50th anniversary. (You can hold your Forrest Gump jokes. I've heard them all.) We would walk and meet with kids in grade schools and Boys & Girls Clubs to extoll the benefits of physical activity, let them know that walking is a great place to start, and encourage them to get their parents to walk with them.

Beginning in New York City on that April morning we walked through New Jersey, Delaware, Maryland, Virginia, West Virginia, Pennsylvania, Ohio, Indiana, Illinois, Missouri, Arkansas, Oklahoma, Texas, New Mexico, Arizona and California. By the time we got to Amarillo, Texas two months and more than 1800 miles later, I had developed a stress fracture in my heel.

At first, I told myself it was nothing. Just a bruise or possibly I had stepped on a rock wrong, so I didn't mention it to anyone and kept walking. But I was walking 20 to 25 miles daily and on the days I wasn't walking I was standing on my feet for 6 to 8 hours every day, and this soon made it worse. It got to the point that with every step I took a shooting pain went all the way up my leg and into my back. Every step required I recommit to my goal.

I could have let the pain stop me. When I told our handlers they said I could stop and someone else would walk for me, but I was committed to my goal. Which meant I would recommit as many times as it took.

I did not want to bail out on this adventure. I was not going to quit on my fellow walkers, and I was certainly not going to fail all those kids I had spoken with. Just as importantly, I wasn't going to fail me.

From the time I was a young boy and learned how to ride a bike I had dreamed of biking across the country. That did not happen, so when this opportunity to walk across the country presented itself, I knew it was for me. This was my YES. I had no idea if I would ever get another opportunity like this and I wasn't going to let it slip away.

Every day I would tell whoever I was walking with, "Once I get started walking, I'm not stopping for anything. Not a snack, not to rest, not to use the bathroom, nothing. The pain is the worst when I first start walking and I am going to just keep rolling so I can honor my commitment."

We had another month and over 1000 miles to go across the deserts of New Mexico, Arizona and California and if I had to recommit every day, every step, to reach the ocean, that's what I was going to do. Remember this was my YES. This wasn't a Maybe, this was divine guidance telling me to stay the course.

YES, I wanted to follow through and keep my word to all those school kids I'd told I was walking to California, but there was something more to this. I was doing this for me. I didn't know how or if what I was doing would inspire any of the people I met along this walk, but I knew it would change me forever.

I shared with you a little bit ago that when I was a little boy, whenever I would say I can't do something my Dad would say "Can't never did anything." Even though I knew he was right, I stayed attached to *can't* for many years. It was my out, my back door escape route when things got hard or went differently than I expected them to.

Can't was my fear of failure winning out over my commitment to success. It would have been so easy to have said "I can't go on!" and quit, but there was no way in hell I was going to let that happen this time.

Walking onto Santa Monica pier on that beautiful July day after all the blisters, sore muscles, wrong turns and the weeks of excruciating pain from my stress fracture, ended my addiction to *can't* forever.

As we approached the final miles we were joined by Olympic gold medalist, and three-time world figure skating champion Peggy Fleming. I was amazed at how excited she was for what we'd done. This was a world champion athlete and she was genuinely impressed with our accomplishment. Once we reached the pier and finished our walk Peggy gave each of us a book, and the inscription she wrote read: "Thank you for all your steps of inspiration!"

Sometimes we sell ourselves short. We don't realize the impact we have by following our YES and committing to being true ourselves. By following a YES I had since childhood I ended up inspiring thousands of kids and an Olympic champion. You just never know.

There is a great passage from a book by Scottish writer and mountaineer W. H. Murray[71] that sums up the importance of committing:

> *Until one is committed, there is hesitancy, the chance to draw back. Concerning all acts of initiative (and creation), there is one elementary truth, the ignorance of which kills countless ideas and splendid plans: that the moment one definitely commits oneself, then Providence moves too. All sorts of things occur to help one that would never otherwise have occurred. A whole stream of events issues from the decision, raising in one's favor all manner of unforeseen incidents and meetings and material assistance, which no man could have dreamed would have come his way. Whatever you can do, or dream you can do, begin it. Boldness has genius, power, and magic in it. Begin it now.*

Be bold, commit to your dreams, follow your YES, recommit as often as needed, and success will meet you wherever you go.

— 35 —

The Invitation

I have an invitation for you. I'm aware that as you read this book you may have been beating yourself up a bit, thinking "I'm not very good at maintaining a practice" or "I'm terrible at doing this kind of thing." We all have this kind of self-talk occasionally, however listening to it leads to what is known as *deficiency motivation*. In other words, thinking you are not enough, incapable, or broken in some way and that you must change in order to fix yourself. The problem with this is it traps us in an endless process of trying to fill the bottomless pit of "not enough."

My invitation to you is to view yourself as complete in the moment. Recognizing you are doing the best you can with what you have right here and right now. No comparisons to what was or what could be. When you approach life in this way it leads to *growth motivation*, where you honor who you are now, and allow yourself to be excited about growing and blooming by following your YES.

A rose does not have to rid itself of its thorns in order to bloom and neither do you. If a rose focused on getting rid of its thorns it would be trapped in deficiency motivation and never bloom. Instead it knows it has thorns, they are just part of life. The rose is excited about growing and blooming because it also knows that once it blooms its thorns become insignificant. We've all pricked our finger on a thorn when picking up a rose, but we didn't care because the magnificence of the rose blossom was worth it.

Let's take a minute now and revisit the question I asked you in Chapter 1 - The Rose.

Which stage of the rose do you see yourself in currently?

- Are you a thorny green plant? A rose bush with no blooms or buds on it? You lack confidence and are indecisive. Your gifts are hidden away, you're uncomfortable fully expressing yourself, and you're a long way from blooming and thriving.
- Are you a budding rose bush? It's clear you have potential. You're better than you used to be at making choices and speaking your truth, but you're still not fully opening and sharing your gifts and your passions with confidence.
- Or are you a fully blooming rose bush? Are you confidently sharing your unique gifts with the world, and no longer doubting yourself? Are you blossoming for no other reason than it is who you are, and as a result are you being admired by many and truly loved by the select few who would bend over backwards to do what it takes to support you in continuing to bloom?

There is nothing wrong with which ever category you find yourself in. Just because you are there today, does not mean you have to stay there forever. No matter which stage you find yourself in, a thorny plant, just starting to bud or fully blooming, following your YES will upgrade your life in more ways than you can imagine. I've witnessed it with 1000s of people over the years and I promise it will be true for you as well.

Following your YES is optional. We all know this because we've not followed our YES before and it didn't kill us. However, when we don't follow our YES we are like the rose that never blooms. We are just a thorny green plant that most people don't pay much attention to and often try to avoid. But that's not what a rose is here for, is it? Our gifts, just like the rose, show up when we bloom and we bloom when we follow our YES.

Allow yourself to live a life of alignment in harmony with your heart and your truth. Trust the divine guidance you receive through your feelings to blossom and expand into your most complete expression. Share your gifts with the world one step at a time.

Now that you've learned about following your YES go do it. Actually look with different eyes, look for the feelings instead of the forms, and release your resistance. Let go of the stories of how it has to look and then take action on those two questions about where you are now and where you want to be.

Following your YES is a life of exploration, curiosity, and opening to new possibilities while knowing full well that the Universe has your back, and it loves to surprise you with things that are just as good as what you thought it would be or even better.

As I mentioned at the beginning of the book, I view you, me and everyone on Earth as roses that are here to bloom. My intention is to help the world be filled with blooming roses. People who are living their fullest expression, who have found their voice, reconnected with their Inner Authority, and are confidently sharing their gifts with the world. This life is available to you when you consistently follow your YES so you can blossom and attract the people, opportunities and experiences that support you in continuing to bloom.

If you are already there, bravo! Keep it going.

If you notice you are not there yet but you want to be and need more support and practice, know I'm here for you. Simply go to:

www.followyouryes.com

and you will find all the resources you need to become a master at following your YES and trusting your guidance so you can bloom and live your best life.

Principles of Following Your YES

* Your YES is a feeling that invites you forward and inspires you to act.
* Your YES is loving and supportive. It is not there to judge you.
* Your YES is always regarding you.
* When you're following your YES you build confidence and eliminate competition.
* Your awareness of what you don't want is the invitation to explore what you do want.
* Don't be afraid of NO; it is actually your friend.
* Maybes happen when we don't trust the Universe is on our side.
* Your YES is always guiding you towards your highest good.
* Risk is a vehicle to expand your world.
* Avoiding what you don't want is never your YES.
* Whatever you put your energy into you will experience.
* Following your YES is listening to your Inner Authority.
* If you want to master following your YES, you need to respect it.
* Your YES is yours, and you don't need to justify it to anyone.
* Being afraid to follow your YES is normal. Do it anyway!

(You can download a printable version of these principles at followyouryes.com/principles)

Acknowledgements

To my many teachers and mentors thank you for seeing more in me than I saw in myself. You have inspired me to follow in your footsteps and do the same for others in order for the world to be filled with blooming roses.

To Patti M. Hall my book diviner, without your encouragement, expertise and enthusiasm to see this book written there's no telling if these pages would have ever come to be. Through your generous guidance I found the confidence to do something I never thought I would do. I was convinced I was not a writer and you helped me see that wasn't true at all.

To the Story House gang - Dr. Erin Baker and Tim Snell this has been a fabulous ride and I couldn't ask for better people to share the journey with.

To the technology gods and Otter.ai who helped me bridge the gap between my whole hearted belief that I was not a writer to being a published author. Your contribution to helping the writing averse be writers anyway is immeasurable.

To everyone who read early drafts of the book and provided candid feedback. Cameron Adibi, Marianne Mallonee, Wendy Gillespie your comments and insights contributed to a much more cohesive message, and I can't thank you enough for providing new eyes through which to view this material.

To the Universe, the Divine, the source of every YES. Your guidance is always on point. Even when I try and avoid it, like resisting writing this book for 6 years, you are steadfast in your support. I'm thrilled to have learned to trust you as my guide.

To my students and clients past, present and future. You are the proof that sharing the message of YES truly is the gift I am here to share with the world. Thank you for your commitment to living your YES, being your best in all you do, and allowing me to play a role by supporting you in fully blooming.

There are many more people who contributed to this book. As much as I'd like to individually thank everyone who helped make this book a reality, I'm aware this is beyond my ability. There are simply too many raindrops that have nourished this rose for me to name them all. So I will say thank you to *all* of you. Whether you touched my life for a few seconds or a few decades, your contribution to me being where I am today is something I cherish.

About the Author

Ken Bechtel is an internationally renowned spiritual teacher, speaker, and author of *Follow Your YES*, who has invested over 20 years in researching and refining what it takes to make room for you to bloom in this busy world. Ken is a minister with decades of experience in helping people connect with their divine guidance. He is the creator and host of the "Finding You In The Goo" radio show and the "Speaking of Partnership" podcast reaching listeners in over 100 countries.

Ken is on a mission to empower you to blossom into your fullest expression from the inside out, so you can live the fulfilling life you came here to live. He is here to help you reclaim your self-confidence personally, professionally and romantically through the power of following your YES.

Ken lives at the foot of the Rocky Mountains in Colorado where you are likely to find him biking around town, frequenting a farmer's market with a hot chai in hand or hiking in the mountains.

Endnotes

1 Sir Richard Branson is the founder of the Virgin Group. - https://www.virgin.com/branson-family/richard-branson

2 The Universe - ©www.tut.com

3 For more on Italian philosopher and theologian St. Thomas Aquinas go to - https://biography.yourdictionary.com/st-thomas-aquinas

4 Judy Garland is an American actress and singer, most famous for playing Dorthy in the Wizard of Oz. - https://www.imdb.com/name/nm0000023/bio?ref_=nm_ov_bio_sm

5 From the book - *You're Born an Original Don't Die a Copy!*

- http://freshword.com/shop/youre-born-an-original-dont-die-a-copy

6 Jay Shetty is a former monk and the author of "Think Like a Monk." To watch the speech where this quote came from go to - https://youtu.be/f61pewuXfPs

7 Seneca was a Roman statesman and stoic philosopher - https://www.worldhistory.org/Seneca/

8 Ingrid Bergman - Swedish actress - https://www.imdb.com/name/nm0000006/bio#overview

9 Michael Bernard Beckwith is a New Thought minister, author, and founder and spiritual director of the Agape International Spiritual Center in Beverly Hills, California - https://michaelbeckwith.com/

10 Listen to my full interview with Jeffrey Allen here - https://speakingofpartnership.com/episodes/072-follow-your-yes-friday-19/

11 Michael Neill is a renowned transformative teacher, author, broadcaster, and speaker. - https://www.michaelneill.org/about/

12 Rex Harrison was an English actor. - https://www.imdb.com/name/nm0001322/

13 *Serious Straw Bale* - https://www.amazon.com/gp/product/1890132640/ref=dbs_a_def_rwt_hsch_vapi_taft_p1_i0

14 Gisele Bundchen is a model, activist and businesswoman. - http://giselebundchen.com/bio/

15 A Return to Love: Reflections on the Principles of A Course in Miracles" by Marianne Williamson. This poem appeared in chapter seven.

16 Full lyrics to "Iris" by the Goo Goo Dolls - https://www.azlyrics.com/lyrics/googoodolls/iris.html

17 Listen to my full interview with Preston Smiles here - https://speakingofpartnership.com/episodes/048-follow-your-yes-friday-11/

18 Wayne Dyer author and speaker in the fields of self-development and spiritual growth. - https://www.drwaynedyer.com/about-dr-wayne-dyer/

19 Mahatma Gandhi is most famous for his philosophy of nonviolence that has inspired civil rights leaders around the world. - https://www.biography.com/activist/mahatma-gandhi

20 Jennifer Price - https://www.jenniferprice.com/about

21 Moss Hart is an American playwright - https://en.wikipedia.org/wiki/Moss_Hart

22 Marsha Sinetar is a pioneering educator. - http://www.marshasinetar.com/about/

23 Barbara Hall is an American television writer and novelist. - https://www.imdb.com/name/nm0355329/?ref_=nmbio_bio_nm

24 Listen to my full interview with Heide Banks here - https://speakingofpartnership.com/episodes/060-follow-your-yes-friday-15/

25 Michael J. Tamura is a Spiritual Teacher, Clairvoyant Visionary, Radio Show Host & Author of *You Are The Answer* - https://www.michaeltamura.com/

26 Anna Marie Quindlen is an American author, journalist, and opinion columnist. - https://www.penguinrandomhouse.com/authors/24734/anna-quindlen/

27 Listen to my full interview with Dr. Laura Ciel - https://speakingofpartnership.com/episodes/051-follow-your-yes-friday-12/

28 Lao-tzu Chinese philosopher and writer. - https://www.worldhistory.org/Lao-Tzu/

29 The Amazing Triple Spiral video can be viewed at - https://www.followyouryes.com/dominos

30 Wayne Dyer author and speaker in the fields of self-development and spiritual growth. - https://www.drwaynedyer.com/about-dr-wayne-dyer/

31 David Bowie was an English singer-songwriter and actor. - https://www.davidbowie.com/about

32 Inc. Magazine online - https://www.inc.com/jessica-stillman/want-to-learn-faster-make-your-life-more-unpredictable.html

33 Steven Pressfield is an American author of historical fiction, non-fiction, and screenplays. - https://en.wikipedia.org/wiki/Steven_Pressfield

34 T. Harv Eker is the author of Secrets of the Millionaire Mind. https://www.amazon.com/gp/product/B000FCJZ3G/ref=dbs_a_def_rwt_bibl_vppi_i0

35 To access the movie Free Solo go here - https://films.nationalgeographic.com/free-solo. Alex Honnold is a professional adventure rock climber. http://www.alexhonnold.com/about#bio

36 To have me walk you through how to expand your comfort zone simply access this guided meditation - followyouryes.com/comfort

37 From the movie Queen of Katwe. - https://www.imdb.com/title/tt4341582/

38 T.S. Eliot was a poet, literary critic, dramatist, and editor, publisher Nobel Prize winner. - https://www.poetryfoundation.org/poets/t-s-eliot

39 Listen to this Ella Fitzgerald recording here - https://youtu.be/6vX-AtVbZbkI

40 Anais Nin was a 20th century diarist. - https://theanaisninfoundation.org/bio

41 Hugh White is the author of Nature And Salvation In Piers Plowman. - https://www.forbes.com/quotes/4480/

42 Karen Salmansohn is a self-help book author. - https://www.notsalmon.com/notsalmon-story/

43 I originally learned this exercise from my friend and mentor Alison Armstrong. You can learn more about her work at - www.alisonarmstrong.com

44 Gay Hendricks is a psychologist, writer, and teacher in the field of personal growth, relationships, and body intelligence. - https://hendricks.com/about/

45 Leon Brown was an outfielder in Major League Baseball. - https://www.overallmotivation.com/quotes/leon-brown-quotes/

46 Phyllis Ann George was an American businesswoman, actress, and sportscaster. - https://en.wikipedia.org/wiki/Phyllis_George

47 Johann Wolfgang von Goethe was a German poet, playwright, and novelist. - https://www.poetryfoundation.org/poets/johann-wolfgang-von-goethe

48 Alice Morse Earle was an American historian and author. - https://www.encyclopedia.com/arts/news-wires-white-papers-and-books/earle-alice-morse

49 Denzel Hayes Washington Jr. is an American actor, director, and producer. - https://www.imdb.com/name/nm0000243/

50 Robert F. Kennedy was an American lawyer and politician. - https://www.jfklibrary.org/learn/about-jfk/the-kennedy-family/robert-f-kennedy

51 Vince Lombardi was an American football coach and executive in the National Football League. - http://www.vincelombardi.com/about.html

52 The HeartMath Institute - https://www.heartmath.org/ View the complete paper - https://www.heartmath.org/assets/uploads/2015/01/the-resonant-heart.pdf

53 Listen to my full interview with Drs. Joy & Roy Martina here - https://speakingofpartnership.com/episodes/011-follow-your-yes-friday-2-bonus-stories-from-this-weeks-guests/

54 Alfred Adler was an Austrian medical doctor, psychotherapist, and founder of the school of individual psychology. - https://www.adler.edu/alfred-adler-history/

55 Alexi Panos is a transformational vlogger, speaker and writer. - www.alexipanos.com

56 Eleanor Roosevelt was an American political figure, diplomat, and activist. - https://www.fdrlibrary.org/er-biography

57 Oprah Winfrey is an American talk show host, television producer, actress, author, and philanthropist. - https://www.biography.com/media-figure/oprah-winfrey

58 From the book "Rising Strongly" by American research professor, lecturer, and author Brene' Brown - https://brenebrown.com/book/rising-strong/

59 Listen to my full interview with Marni Battista here - https://speakingofpartnership.com/episodes/039-follow-yes-friday-8/

60 Thích Nhất Hạnh was a Vietnamese Thiền Buddhist monk, peace activist, prolific author, poet, and teacher. - https://thichnhathanhfoundation.org/thich-nhat-hanh

61 Vincent Willem van Gogh was a Dutch Post-Impressionist painter. https://www.vincentvangogh.org/biography.jsp

62 Avram J. Holmes, Lauren M. Patrick. The Myth of Optimality in Clinical Neuroscience. Trends in Cognitive Sciences, 2018; DOI: 10.1016/j.tics.2017.12.006 - https://www.sciencedaily.com/releases/2018/02/180220123129.htm

63 Quote from "True Love: Stories Told To and By Robert Fulghum." https://www.robertleefulghum.com/aboutrobert

64 For more on Mihaly Csikszentmihalyi and the concept of flow go to - https://www.famouspsychologists.org/mihaly-csikszentmihalyi/

65 For more on American singer, songwriter, and dancer Michael Jackson go to - https://www.biography.com/musician/michael-jackson

66 Sir Richard Starkey MBE, better known by his stage name Ringo Starr, is an English musician, singer, songwriter and actor who achieved international fame as the drummer for the Beatles. - https://www.ringostarr.com/about

67 Maya Angelou was an American poet, memoirist, and civil rights activist. - https://www.mayaangelou.com/biography/

68 Jules Lederer was an American business executive and innovator. https://en.wikipedia.org/wiki/Jules_Lederer

69 The Universe - ©www.tut.com

70 Marc Von Musser is a sales expert, consultant and trainer. - https://www.linkedin.com/in/marcvonmusser/

71 William H. Murray was a Scottish mountaineer and writer. - https://www.undiscoveredscotland.co.uk/usbiography/m/whmurray.html

Printed in Great Britain
by Amazon